An Arrow In My Heart
A FIRST NATION WOMAN'S ACCOUNT OF SURVIVAL FROM THE STREETS TO THE HEIGHT OF ACADEMIA

Sharon L. Acoose, PhD

3104 30th Ave., Suite 228
Vernon, BC V1T 9M9

www.jcharltonpublishing.com

JCharlton Publishing Ltd.
3104 30th Ave., Suite 228
Vernon, BC Canada
V1T-9M9

www.jcharltonpublishing.com

Copyright © 2015 JCharlton Publishing Ltd. All rights reserved. No part of this publication may be photocopied, reproduced, stored in a retrieval system, or transmitted, in any form or by any means, electronic, mechanical or otherwise, without the written permission of JCharlton Publishing Ltd., except for brief passages quoted for review purposes.

Cover picture © Sharon Acoose
Photographs pp. 9, 13, 32, 46, 56, 85, 96, 101 © Sharon Acoose.

Library and Archives Canada Cataloguing in Publication

Acoose, Sharon, author
    An arrow in my heart : a First Nations woman's account of survival from the streets to the height of academia / Sharon Acoose.

Includes bibliographical references.
ISBN 978-1-926476-01-8 (pbk.)

1. Acoose, Sharon. 2. Native peoples--Canada--Biography.
3. Women college teachers--Canada--Biography. 4. First Nations University of Canada--Faculty--Biography. I. Title.

E90.A26A3 2015   971.004'970092   C2015-900101-3

ACKNOWLEDGEMENTS

Acknowledgements

*F*irst and foremost I want to acknowledge a Creator of my understanding for holding me up when I could not hold myself up. Mikwec. I will forever be in my Creator's debt for showing me that there is another way to live. I surrendered and I let the Creator work his magic. My soul is clean my heart is clean and every day I am blessed with life I say it like it is. *Mikwec*!

DEDICATION

Dedication

I am dedicating this book to my pops Joseph Gabriel Acoose and my moms Olive Acoose (Pelletiter). Both my parents are deceased but really they have been living in my heart I just didn't know it. I had to sober up to understand and realized although they both passed on they have never really left me. I am never Alone! None of us are!

I also want to dedicate this book to my only living brother Gerald W. Acoose and his wife Lynda Acoose who have been my silent rocks through all my craziness and in my success. *Mikwec*!

TABLE OF CONTENTS

Table of Contents

Acknowledgements — i
Dedication — v

Chapter 1: Introduction — 1
Kiishiibii-biizun Kineu Ikue (Cirlcing Eagle Woman) 3

Chapter 2: Arrow In My Heart — 5
Memories of Childhood Sexual Abuse 7
My Pops 9
My Moms 13
More Stories of Youth and Mayhem 18
Sexual Abuse: the Suffering of a Child 22

Chapter 3: Years Into The Darkness — 29
The Arrow in my Heart: My Descent into a
   Life of Drugs, Alcohol, and Prostitution 33

Chapter 4: More Rigorous Adventures Of My Life On The Street — 39
My Family Affairs 42
My Sister 45
The Eve's of Junior 45

Chapter 5: Life In Jail: A World All It's Own — 49

Chapter 6: More Tales Of Woe From The Dark Side — 65
A Drug Deal Gone Wrong 76
My Baby Boy 76

Chapter 7: The Arrow In My Heart... Disappears — 81
The Other Side of Jail 85
The Cherry on Top of the Cake 93
The Beginning 96

About The Author — 99

Pictures:
My pops in his truck 9
My mom and dad 13
Me at 13 32
Me at 17 34
Star (my daughter) 46
Me at 20 56

Table of Contents

Me at 45 85
Me at 61 96
My PhD grad photo 101

CHAPTER 1

Introduction

Introduction

The story I am about to share is based on the facts of my life. I will discuss what I used to be like, what happened in my life, and where I am today. I have followed some simple rules, guidelines, and teachings from Indian Elders. I learned everything by trial and error. I came, I saw, and I conquered. I rose from the ashes to where I am at this moment. I lived through extreme pain and suffering. I never thought I would live to see twenty years of age, but here I am sixty-one, and I am still rocking. Like so many other alcoholics and drug addicts who have come out the other end triumphant, my life story is a miracle. I have learned to serve a Creator of my understanding. I have come to believe, in a power higher than myself for once in my life. This is my healing journey from nowhere land. And for once in all I will take the arrow from my heart.

Kiishiibii-biizuu Kinew Ikwe (Circling Eagle Woman)

Anin sikwa, I am Circling Eagle Woman—this is my Indian name. I was given my Indian name by (Elder) Dr. Danny Musqua. My Christian name is Sharon Leslie Acoose. I was born May 3rd, 1953 in Regina, Saskatchewan. 1953—yup that was a good year! I am going to be sharing bits, pieces, and parts of my healing journey and life story with you. I am going to do storytelling with you, which in the Indian way is a form of sharing one's own life. It can also be called oral storytelling. I have learned that it is not just our Elders who do oral storytelling—anyone who has lived and has something of significance to share, whether an individual or a group, can do oral storytelling. Mine is a story of pain, misery, and agony. I am going to share my experience, strength and hope with you. I will talk about my past life, where it took me and about how I managed to turn failures into a series of successes.

The change has been drastic but necessary. I have sat idle far too long. You will hear about hurdle after hurdle that I had to get over and crosses I had to bear; but it will be positive. Well most of it I think, but one never knows. I realize there are many inspiring stories on the shelves and that I am not unique. However, if there is one person who reads this book and survives because of something I say then it will all have been worth the struggle. I also am glad to see this story being published for the world to see. This book is written with the hope that a fellow addict catches something and finds peace and harmony for their lives. Even if you do not have alcohol/drug problems, I am sure you will still find something to make you feel better about yourself. I mean really, not all people are addicts but we all have some kind of worry. We all have a few ghosts hanging out that need to be subdued and loved back to whatever it is we need. It is my hope that you all understand, feel, and know that you do have a choice no matter what you do in your life and that only you can make the appropriate choice(s). From these pages, within the ink upon them, there is hope. With every stroke on the keyboard there are years of pain being washed away and there is a joy that is overwhelming. I am lost and desolate no more. Elated and heavenly are the feelings that pump through my veins straight to my heart into yours. Here is my story.

CHAPTER 2

Arrow In My Heart

Life was not easy. I was born and so I had to live. What I have today I never thought conceivable? I figured my life was going to be short. So many times I attempted to end this life but there was something that always saved my sorry ass. It was my destiny. I was meant not to perish. I was meant to be at the place where I am. I believe in fate and this is mine. The ghosts are ready to be spoken about and diminished. I am ready and so is the child that was hidden for so many lost years. The silence is gone and my voice is clear. My will to live and my passion are my new choices in life. I also do not force anyone to listen. I make no bones about my past and I will tell anyone who wants to hear. I call a spade a spade. I will say whatever has to be said without hurting another. There have been many obstacles in my path but I made it through, over, under, and around most of them. It was like I was possessed to succeed. The thought of failing just freaked me out. I could feel it in the tip of my toes to the top of my head. There was an unknown force that motivated me to do the best that I could and this is all that I have done, my best, no more no less. The darkness is gone. The shadows are no longer freaky. The light shines through tenfold. The sun shines gloriously if you will. I no longer feel the need to turn to alcohol and drugs. Well okay there are moments when a Cold One or just a 'little jimmy' would do the trick, but I fight it and move on. I search in other places for the comfort that I need. I was gonna say I was still afraid of the dark but I am not, that ship too has sailed. I have dealt with my demons and I have let go and let the Creator into my life.

I never knew how to act or talk or think or understand or listen or anything. It was too hard and I cared not to know. I just wanted to be left alone and not be bothered. I was ashamed of who I was and what I did as a child or what was done to me as a child. Then I carried that into my adolescents and through to adulthood. Whatever, my wrath always led to violence and this would be my biggest downfall. I have so many memories that are flooding through my mind. I have wanted to do this for so long but just never got around to it for one reason or another. It's been a long life so bear with me. I lived in Regina during most of my youth. My family moved off the Sakimay Indian Reservation back in the early 1950s. I would be born into a world that would not be kind to me. It would be dark, as my life would become. This life I have lived is mine, and like many other addicts I do not hold anyone responsible except myself. I did the things I did to survive. It is the only way I knew how to exist. There were those who would steal my soul, and you will meet them as you read on.

Memories of Childhood Sexual Abuse
I am not sure where to begin because right now my mind is swimming

with old memories, old ghosts walking, of the past gone by. I knew once I began this would happen but it's all-good, and we will get through it one very emotional moment at a time. There is much to explore. So many adventures I have seen. So many intimate moments I have had. We will just leave it natural and uncensored. We will see as we go along. I do not think it will be me that makes the last decision of how it will be edited, but that is cool. It really does not matter. I am taking the chance writing it. It is my healing journey. At least I am taking the risk—and it's a healthy risk. It is the only way that I am able to stay clean and serene. Now that I have had the chance to think this through, I know it will not be easy because the ghosts have many hurtful memories. But that is the point, to get through and to feel again on a more normal level per se. This is important. My journey has only just begun and I look forward to sharing it with you. If, well never mind if, you will run into some harsh lingo so please do not be offended because it is not meant to hurt you. Maybe once I am done the editors will help me or perhaps after they read it they will know and just leave it as is. These are only words. Warning, if you take things said too personally, then just don't read what I have to say. If you think you can handle this story, and some harsh words, then all the power to you.

By the time I was three years of age my life was pretty much tangled and mangled. When I first sobered up I only remembered a certain amount of events from five years of age on. However, as my sobriety progressed, so did my memories. I remember working nights as a jail guard and this is where I started keeping a journal, which was where my idea of a book was born. And as my thoughts progressed more ghosts began to filter through, and my earliest recollection of things move further back to the age of three. I do not remember all things from this age, however, there are some things that really stick out quite vividly. I remember feeling afraid all of the time and I never really knew why. There were always plenty of people around and sometimes there were not. My parents – like myself, did not have strong parenting skills. However, at the time and place there were not too many agencies that anyone could reach out to. Essentially you were on your own. My parents did the best they could with what they had at the time. God rest their beautiful souls. You know back in the 50's it was rough stuff especially for Indian people and that we were. My dad left the Reserve, I assume, to give us a better life. You know I really am not sure why he left but he did. I do know that he was forced to sell his Treaty Rights and the Treaty Rights of our family. That was one of the "fair" government's lame attempts to assimilate/colonize us. Back then, when an Indian left the Reservation they had to give up those Treaty Rights. My dad didn't know he was not educated and so he would sell his families Treaty Rights so that he could live and prosper

Arrow in my Heart

in Regina. My dad always did work, this I remember. I think if he had known for sure how life would be he would have stayed put on the Rez.

He drove a big truck for Regina Cartage and Storage. He did provide for us as any father would. My dad did not know that drinking was going to be such a big deterrent for our whole family. If had, I'm sure circumstances would have been different, way different. Who is to know or to say for sure? We did not fare well in Regina, any of us, and we would all meet the wrath of the Streets at different stage of our lives.

My Pops

My father, Joseph Gabriel Acoose was the last of my immediate family members to pass on. I was thirty years old when he died. I am using his name because I really do not think he would mind. Besides it is not about my family, it is about me mourning for them, as I should have years ago. And, they are also deserving of recognition because they are my beloved family. My family was as messed up as I was back in the day. It was one disaster after the next. I will not say anything that will hurt my family. All I want is to be able to forgive myself for not being the kind of wife, daughter and sister I should have been or could have been. I owe them that. I owe of them my life! I remember too he walked with a limp. Back in his prime, while on the job, he had stepped on a railroad spike. Not sure what happened but he got gangrene and had to have half of his foot cut off, and I remember the operation was in Montana. I remember moms talking about it to someone and she was concerned. I remember that. Pops would be in the bar and he would be sitting there with his damn shoe turned around backwards and he would get up and walk *dayum* that was funny. I remember that. Every welfare cheque he would buy KFC, you could bank on it. We would feast. He got real mad at me once. I was fixing Seconals in his basement and I did too many. I went into the chills and I was crying and he yelled at me. That was the first and last time my pops ever yelled

An Arrow In My Heart

at me. I was his Angel, his baby who could do no wrong. Ok the Seconals were a sleeping pill or nerve pill but if you cooked it and put it in a needle it had quite the effect. He told me that I shouldn't be doing that damn stuff and sent me to bed. He got over it and I kept using. He made the best pork hocks and white bean soup. He looked after his dad *Mushum King* until he passed away. I do not have too many childhood memories of my pops but what I have I will cherish forever.

Pops was always willing to help anyone. And he was very tidy and kept a clean home. I used to love going there because you could always find food, drink and him. He went to the Marion Center all the time and would bring all kinds of grub back. He had a nickname too and it was *Muckoose*. That was what everybody called him. I remember sitting on his knee and he would bounce me and sing, "*Subba dee dee, subba dee, dee, subba doo, doo subba doo, doo.*" To this day I have no idea what the hell that meant, but it was his song to me. I was his baby girl.

Looking back, I remember coming home—I was living in Prince Albert at the time—for Christmas. I was putting off going to visit my pops and I will regret this for the rest of my life. But not in a way that will hinder my healing. I have already dealt with that pain. We had planned to pick up pops and bring him over for the Christmas meal anyway so I could see him then. He was not going anywhere or so I thought. Little did I know, I would never see my dad alive again. It was December 19th, 1983 when the phone rang. Either that or someone came over and told us; I am not really sure on this. Anyway, whatever, we were told that our father-pops had just died and that one of us had to go identify the body. This is really hard even now as I sit here and type. Identify the body of the man who brought me into this world and of which I could not get off my sorry ass to go visit. Yep it was just messed up is all. I was a fucking hero alright. I am not sure what decisions were made but I ended up going to see my dad for one last time – ever. As things were unfolding, all I could think of was getting high to deal with this pain. Yes, that was always the easiest way for me, I was weak. I wanted to erase my feelings, thoughts, emotions, God help me if I should feel. Yeah, and where the fuck was this so called God? I had to get rid of the pain in my heart, in my soul. I had to deaden my reasoning, my emotions, and whatever else there was to erase. Everything about me was limited, the pain, the misery, the emotions or whatever because as soon as shit came down I got as high as I possibly could.

I immediately got dressed and went to the hospital. When I got there no one was around. I think my dad's woman and her kids were there but that was it. No one else from my family was there and I mean his brothers or whoever, not one was there. It was hard to swallow because he was alone. We just all had way too much stuff of our own I guess. What wicked ways we had. Well at least my dad's woman was there. You have to give her credit. Really, she stood by him thick and thin. I remember her, and she was alright. I asked the nurse where they had my dad and she told me. She also told me I should not go in alone, that I should wait for a doctor or someone else for support. But y'all know how well I listened to anyone. I went in and I will never forget what I saw; ever, fucking ever. It will stay in my memories forever. I found the room and there lay my pops lifeless with a black rubber thing sticking out of his mouth. I remember I was holding him; he was still sort of warm because he had just died and God I felt hopeless. I never felt so fucking hopeless in all my useless days. He was gone. My pops was dead. He left his baby girl all alone in a cold harsh uncaring world. My pops was there with me in the room but only one of us would walk out, and at that moment I wished it could have been him. I never wanted so much to just be dead, gone, deceased. But my scank ass was still alive. I always wanted to be dead this wasn't new. Fuck I hated myself at that moment. I just could not go through this. It was too hard. I prayed for death there in that room with my pops. I just fucking wished the earth would open up her womb and swallow me whole. I wanted death because I was not worthy to live.

    I remember standing there and just looking at him lying on that stretcher. It was so surreal. I was talking to him and sobbing from my heart. I stood there and I just stared at him. I touched that black rubber hose and tried to take it out so that he could talk to me. Oh my God, what have I done? Why am I standing here looking at my dead pops? God had taken all the good ones and left the rubbish behind. They had attempted to save his life but it was his time. He had to go. Naturally I cried but it was not for my father, no it was for me. Sound familiar. Yeah I bet it does. I don't know how long I stayed in that room but it was a long time because my pops had begun to get cold. I laid over him, held onto him and cried. I wanted so badly for him to wake up, we had to go home. We had a Christmas feast to attend. At one point I asked the nurse to get more blankets because my pops was cold. She did just to humor me and I covered him up. They knew I was on the edge or close to it.

    My pops died alone. He died I am sure in pain because heart attacks are not easy. I have never had one but I have heard they are painful. You know I even thought, "Oh great another Christmas ruined, now what?" It was not about my pops, it was about poor Sharon. You know I was hopeless, just hopeless. I went through a funeral with people feeling sorry for me because my pops had died. I sucked it up like the lizard I was. It was never about the death of my loved one because I was never taught how to mourn properly. I mean, I figured you were just supposed to drink or do dope to hide the pain. It would work but only for a while so I merely stayed high for years and years. I would dull my senses and walk in a world full of pain and discontent. And, of all places to die, my pops went down in a Safeway store. He had been sick with heart problems prior to this, but I never came down to see him. I wouldn't do anything that thoughtful. But, I would travel to and from Regina to just get laid, nice. I was such a wonderful caring daughter. I do not remember the last time I seen my father and now I would never see him again. I will never forget him lying in that cold sterile hospital room with a big rubber object sticking out of his mouth. I was fucking devastated, but had no idea how to express it. He was my heart and soul. Yet, at the time I did not know this. So anyway my father would fall to his death in a Safeway store alone. What a fucking travesty and I would walk away with yet another death to bury in my closet. Another excuse for me to get high or drunk or a combination and so I would. It did not really matter, whatever. I hated God. I would renounce God and pray to the devil. He/she would become my God my only God. I hated God with all I had. How could He keep taking the people I loved most in the whole world? What was He fucking stupid or what? Why could He just not take me and let my family come back. I had no idea at all how to deal with all this. The pain I lived with was insurmountable. It was in the very core of my being. I could almost feel it throbbing in my seams.

The more I thought about it the deeper the pain embedded itself into my veins, in my heart and in my mind. There was no other way for me to go. I was like a sitting duck. I was so afraid and so alone. My skills were extremely limited. All I could think about was me. I never thought for a moment that my eldest brother might need some support or comforting. No it was all about me, nothing more. How could God do this to poor Sharon? So I would push this God out of my life forever, almost. Little did I know God would linger just waiting for me to snap out of it. However, as far as I was concerned God was dead, as dead as my pops. He was the enemy. We were now officially at war. God was on the other side.

I lived like this for a long time. I never really felt for anyone who died. Perhaps I did but it hurt too much so I handled it my way. I put them behind me, way behind me, and moved on through life unconsciously. And, once again, I drank through yet another funeral without care or compassion. Come to think of it, I cannot even remember my father's funeral. Nothing, I do not remember a thing, and for this I have suffered every day of my life, and for this I am sorry so very sorry. I do not even know if I gave comfort to my dad's lady friend. She was not my mother so why should I care. What did it matter that she stood by him for more than twenty-five years. So what if she loved my dad without condition? Who cared, not me. She was not my mother. She was nothing in my eyes. I was ruthless. My dad loved this woman and really that is all that counted. Who was I to condemn her? At least she was with him at the hospital after he passed on. I think at one point she and pops had made arrangements to marry, but that never happened. He was buried and I would move on without looking back. I went back to Prince Albert and got even more stoned. I moved through life with no inhibitions or motivations. I just went slowly and sadly. I would continue to stash all my emotions in the coffins we buried my family members in. I was dead. God would be my enemy for years to come.

What are morals? What is appreciation? Where does love go when a loved one dies? What? What does this all mean? I have no answers and may never know. However, I have common sense, and at this moment I know that mistakes have to be made in order to learn to have most of your questions fulfilled. How do you let go of something that you have loved so much? How do you forget the past and move on? Well you never will forget and you will learn to handle it no matter how difficult it may be. Forgetting is not the answer. Forgiving yourself is the key. Not even forgiving others, but just forgiving yourself and then letting go will become easier for you to do.

My Moms

What can I say about my moms? I can see my moms. It is such a nice feeling. Sad once in a while because at one point I could not remember what my mom looked like – but only for a moment – and then she came back. I remembered and it made me cry. I can see her now and the others who have passed on and moved into the next world. I do not think there is a Heaven, but there has to be somewhere and wherever that is, my people are there watching, guiding and taking care of me spiritually. This I believe. They were all so beautiful and so dearly missed. I am so glad to have these thoughts. I am so glad to have these remnants of these beautiful ghosts of the past gone by. At long last I am able to share the joys, the ghosts, and all the feelings that have been lying dormant in my soul. At last.

I can remember my mom trying so hard to be a good parent to my brother's, my sister and me. She could see no wrong in the way we lived – her children. You know she use to wash our clothes, iron them, cleaned for us and cooked our meals. She was something else I tell you. I remember she did complain but nonetheless she loved us without condition. She would have done anything for us and she did, after all we were her babies' right up until the day she left us. These people – my family, were my foundation, but that foundation slowly, meticulously fell askew through the absoluteness of alcohol and drugs. I am not sure, but I do believe that my father had alcohol stuff going on. But I mean I cannot say for sure. I do remember that he was a tad violent back in the day. There were times when my moms would meet his wrath, as did my brothers, as did, I am sure, my sister. But never me, I was the baby.

My moms did everything for me. She was this lil power tank and she said what had to be said. I remember when I was young she drank but towards the end of her life I didn't see it so much. She never did drugs that I knew of. She was a housewife and she did housewife things. I remember she did laundry and man it was, honestly, the whitest on the block. This was before automatic shit and she had a state of the art Winger Washer; the best back then. She had a big ass steel bin beside that washer and the water was blue. That is how moms got the clothes so shiny white. I never heard her complaining about housework. I remember one time she went to visit my sister in Winnipeg. I was maybe fourteen and she left me alone but I think that my brothers might have been there but I know I was there. So, I decided to have some friends over. One of them brought over a huge ass bottle of vanilla extract and they sent me to the store to get some Coke-a-cola. This was the first and last time I ever drank vanilla extract and coke. But dayum we got drunk! It was gross tasting but kids will be kids, right? I also ended up with the hangover of all hangovers, that shit was some powerful. When moms got back, she asked me if I'd been baking because all you could sell was the vanilla extract, so I said yes. She never gave me heck just accepted my insanity and loved me without condition.

Another time, when I was fifteen and had been out all night getting high on LSD, I got home early in the morning. I was sneaking and slithering around the house like the snake I was trying to be quiet. I was so stoned. I'm in the bathroom getting ready for school and I was having a hard time as I was laughing at myself because I was an idiot. Moms comes to the door and gently tells me to hurry up or I'd be late for school. In all my ignorance I yelled, "Oh fuck off leave and me alone!" It went quiet and the next thing you know that bathroom door fly's open and there she is, broom in hand. Well I got a well deserved beating in that bathtub, but I will tell you that I never swore at her again. I didn't respect her either, but that's how I rolled.

I remember a Christmas when I was about thirteen. I was so excited because I had the biggest gift under the tree and it was from my moms. Come Christmas Day I attacked that big ass gift with all the might I had—and then, I sat there in utter disgust. I did not show it of course because it was from moms. It was the ugliest red corduroy coat with a fake fur collar that you could ever imagine. My brother was rolling around on the floor laughing like the fool he was. I was heartbroken. But I sucked it up and told my mom that it was the most beautiful thing in the world—and in the end I think I wore it twice. If she would ask me why I was not wearing it, I would make up some lame-ass excuse, and being the gem she was, she believed me. That coat would stay on the hanger and look new forever. I do remember a few Christmases where I would buy my brothers the same thing every year—Brut cologne—and I think they just acted surprised to make me feel good. Yup, every year they got the same thing. There were some good times amongst the mayhem.

By the time I hit thirteen I'd lost my mind and I was pretty messed up. No one knew, or I do not think anyone knew. I am not even sure if my mom knew what I was; my niece figures she did, but I have no idea. I would be speculating on what someone else says so I just will say I have no idea if she knew what I had become and it's ok. I started smoking cigarettes, smoking dope, and drinking with my friends who were all white. I was the only little Indian girl in my class, and for that matter there were maybe six of us in the whole school back in the day. You have to remember that we were colonized, but that is a story for other books. I am just telling you like it was. My white friends' parents did not like me, but my mom, well she accepted them all into our home. So my house would become a little hang out where we would smoke and try to be kids. We would all hang out in the kitchen in the morning before school to smoke. My mom would kick us out because you couldn't see through the haze. It was funny; you had to be there to experience the moment. I remember once my mom let me have a party for my fifteenth birthday. I invited my buddies and some jackass brought some whiskey and spiked the punch. It was rather tasty if I do say so myself. But booze and fifteen year old kids do not work, and we found that out the hard way that day. We were all dancing, hooting and hollering just having a happy time. My mom kept the goods coming and had no idea that we were drinking booze. Kids kept coming over and we kept on drinking, eating and making merry.

We were having the time of our lives and then it happened. One of my amigos went flying backwards right through the living room picture window. Crash, bang, down she went. Needless to say the party was over. Glass went flying all over the place and kids scattered like ants when their anthill was being squashed. I thought, "Oh my god, oh my god no my mom is gonna kill me". And my beautiful mom didn't even stay mad at me for very long. I got a good scolding and was grounded, but that was it. She was an angel in disguise. She even had two charge accounts for me at clothing stores in Regina back at the time. I mean I got everything I wanted and then some whether I needed it for not. This one time she gave me thirty dollars to go buy shoes. I was a hippy in those days too. I went to a hippy type head shop and bought my shoes and went home. Well my Moms was not too happy I must say. I had bought a pair of hippy sandals that I paid nearly the whole thirty bucks for. I liked them but moms didn't! She would be ok after awhile as always. She was my she-ro!

Another time I was brought home by the police for being extremely drunk. One of my best friend's parents had gone out of town for the weekend so she invited a few of us over. Her parents didn't like me cause I was an Indian, but my friend liked me because I was crazier than a bag of squirrels. We were having fun just trynna be young and wild. The music was loud, the boys started to show up and shit was about to get real. There were a few bottles of Lemon Gin in the fridge and we started drinking it. Before ya knew it we are all bent, me worst of all be-cause I drank by far the most of course. I remember sitting on the couch and I puked. It was like a bloody fountain. My buddy was screaming and other kids were laughing, but I don't remember too much after that but being dragged out by the cops. My friend had to call them cops because we didn't drive, so someone had to get me home. Man I was sick for days after that one and my mom tried to ground me. I knew she was mad at me but she never stayed that way for too long.

I remember when my moms tried to talk to me about having sex. I was disgusted. I got mad at her and said no I wasn't having sex and I wasn't, not at fifteen. But I was getting very close; very close. Anyway, I told her to forget about it and changed the conversation. She was only trying to be a mother to a fucked up insane teenager. She was trying to protect me from myself but that didn't work so well for me. Anyway, the next conversation was when I was seventeen and we were sitting at the kitchen table eating. Moms said, "My girl?" Me, "Yes." Moms, "Are you pregnant?" Me, "Yes" and I nearly choked on what I was eating. I started to cry. I knew I was knocked-up and was trying to figure out how to tell her. She didn't do anything. I didn't get shit. She didn't say, "See I told you so." She just loved me without condition and started to make plans for this baby, unbeknownst to her that she would die. She bent over backwards for me. She cooked, she cleaned and she pampered me. I asked her how she knew and she explained to me that it was in my eyez. She could tell I was pregnant by just looking into my eyez.

My mother died when I was eighteen years of age. She had cancer but I hear tell it wasn't the cancer per se but rather she had gotten ill in the hospital. The last time she went in she didn't come home. That was December 31st, 1970. She was great. Man she did for me what no other person had ever done. She looked after me as best as she could with the resources that she had. She was my rock. I just didn't know it at that time. You know I don't remember telling her that I loved her except when I wanted something. I remember she used to get these wicked diet pills and I would steal them and get high. I would blame my brother and he would get hell for those missing pills.

There was also this lil broad by the name of Elaine Dumba; she's actually on the list of missing/murdered women. She was a lil white girl and we stuck like glue. I am not sure how I met her but I was pregnant so I was sixteen and she was fourteen. Her mother didn't like Indians so of course who did Elaine gravitate to? Indians! She had run away from home and of course my moms would let her stay with us and I think that my moms actually got help from the welfare for her too. I remember I would get mad at Elaine because moms would give her money to go to the store and the bitch wouldn't cut me in. She lived with us for a while and ended up going back home. I remember going to her place and I think her mom had changed her attitude because she liked me. But then again I was Sharon Acoose who wouldn't like me, right? Elaine was part of my family and she called my moms her mom and we accepted her. She was my lil sista. My moms loved Elaine like her real daughter, but she was cool like that.

Then moms would pass on, and the day she passed I was out getting loaded cause it was New Years Eve, 1970. I woke up at my sister's sicker than a dog and someone phoned us to tell us she had passed before midnight. Oh my god I was floored… my first death to deal with. My brother died a few years later so she was the first. I am not sure what happened all I know is the focus was on me and I dug that. It was all about poor little Sharon and man I sucked it all up. People were all over me with pity and I ate it up like there was no tomorrow. Let's back up a moment. My mom ended up with this old dude that my brothers used to tease me about. They'd tell me that he was really my dad and I would get so mad. He had a hair lip and I hated his ass. I remember one time we lived in a trailer court in Regina and one of his son's tried to have sex with me, I was maybe ten, but I was already schooled in this area and it wasn't going to happen. I'd already bumped hip to this shit and no man would ever fuck with me again, so I was able to ward off this stupid kid because really he was only a few years older than me the creep. This old white dude, my mom's man was gross. He would ask me how my vulva felt. I had no idea at the time that he was talking about my vagina. He was so fucked. He asked me once for a pair of my dirty bloomers. Like for fucking real, what was wrong with this picture? He was always giving me money too, but remember now, I was hip to his actions and he would not get shit from me. I was already too wise. I would do my best not to be alone with him. Anyway, I was living with my mom, him and my Granny, my mom's mom, at the last house she would ever live in before her death. My mom had gotten me a bed and made me a little crib in the basement. She was already in the hospital. I came staggering home one night and snuck my way to the basement. I was passing out and I thought I was dreaming. I could feel my bloomers being pulled at and I thought oh fuck that is woah... and then I felt fingers and then I sat straight up in bed and there was this old pervert trying to hand me twenty bucks. He was trying to have sex with me. I pulled out my trusty knife from under my pillow, grabbed him by the collar and said, "If you ever fuck with me again, I will stab you in your black heart!" He tried to say he would tell my moms what I was and I pushed that knife to his throat, but he got away and slithered back up the stairs. That was the last time I ever saw him. I found out years later that he was nothing but a trick and the whole time my Moms was dying. He was paying for sex. My beautiful moms left me to the horrors of a world where time and again an arrow would be in my heart. I heard he married someone my family knew and he died, end of that story.

My parents were vessels of my life. They gave me life and I know that they have never left me. Those vessels would be shattered but I have learned to accept their deaths. My parents didn't know what life had in store for any of us and I cannot even say what might have happened if they did know. It was our destiny to live extreme and, for some of us, to die young. I have written them each a letter to tell them how sorry I was for being such a horrible child and that I love them dearly. They are in my Heart and Soul.

More Stories of Youth and Mayhem
I had a sister ten years my senior, and two older brother's. I remember them but not so much when I was little but more after I got older. My sister left home, why I cannot say for sure. I do know that she lived a hard life, but it's not my story to share. All I know is she tried to look after me, she always gave me a home when needed, but I was too fargone. I cannot blame any of what I did on my family like I hear so many others doing. Suck it up people and take responsibility for your own dumbass actions. I really don't like it when people blame their moms and pops for everything.

Let's stray for a moment. I remember I was sitting out back by the outhouse. This was shortly after I had discovered I was all-alone. I got home from school and no one was there. The house was empty. I was waiting but I am not sure for what or who. I was crying as usual and feeling sick in my little shattered heart; I was only six years old at the time. I could hear someone calling me and I looked up. I remember, for a single fleeting moment feeling happy. I looked up and thought I seen my mommy – but it was not my mommy, it was my aunt, my moms sister. In their younger days they could have passed as twins. I realized it was not my mommy and the balloon popped. My heart again was severely broken, shattered, and I could not stop weeping. I was hopeless and desolate. What else was a six year old to feel? My life was done. All the people I loved dearly in my life had disappeared just like that. The doors just kept slamming shut and I did not know how to open them. After all I was only six. I mean how do you possibly explain at six years of age the grown up feelings that I was experiencing? I was an empty shell and that was the way it would be for a long time, a very long time to come. From that point on everyone took it upon themselves to make all my decisions for me. I ended up in a place run my nuns, and they were some pretty mean bitches I tell you. Obviously they did not know anything about childcare. They did things merely by trial and error; mostly by error I might add. I remember my hair was long and they cut it. I think I had bugs or something bizarre. I never understood any of it, I just accepted and moved on. I was told it was easier for them to deal with short hair and that I'd not look so savage.

    I remember the kids all looking fearful. We were a mix of white and brown kids. We all got beatings well more like strappings for sure. If we had dirty nails, if we did not dress fast enough, or if we refused to eat we would just get it and get it hard. We always got roughed up with a yardstick or one of those thick black straps they had back in those days. It was very traumatizing to say the least. Those nuns were very mean to us and did bizarre shit to all of us. We never went against what the nuns told us. You tired of the beatings after a while and really there was never anyone around to see them hit us. They did it in private and it was not only the little Indian kids that got it, but the white kids as well. I do not remember if I made any friends at this place, but there were always plenty of kids to play with. Those nuns ruled us all. It was very lonely to say the least. I actually remember getting the strap in Grade 8 too and damn that hurt!

    I know that the nuns did call me a 'Lil Savage' when no one was around. At the time I had no idea what they meant by that. I also remember one of them saying that said she was gonna wash the brown off of me. But again no one ever heard. As a child I never understood the concept of racism but I know I lived with it. I kind of figured I was different but I had no idea why or what it meant to be brown. Not only did I suffer all forms of abuse, there was also a slight form of racism at hand. As I sit and write I finally dig the way shit goes. However, it has taken a seriously long time to get a grip on the situation. You know the mind is indeed a powerful tool and it has held me together like glue, thank the Lord. I mean if I were not meant to be here would I be? I think not. It all makes sense to me now. As my life has unfolded before me it finally all makes sense. For so long I have lived in the shadows of time. It was like being on the inside of a mirror looking out trying hard to break through the glass. It seemed the harder I tried to get through the thicker the glass became. It was like trying to dig your way out of a closed coffin that was in the ground. There was no way out, none. I was stuck.

Another thing that sticks out in my mind is that we had to pray day-in and day-out. I remember praying my ass off hoping that I would be rescued from this place, but my prayers would not be answered. We had to pray for everything and I had no idea why or even how to pray. I remember a little white girl told me a prayer so I thought to myself this is the one I would say when it was my turn. So I stood up at the head of the class and I was ready to say my stuff. We all bow our heads and I proceed to go for it. I said, "Hail Mary full of Grace all the chickens had a race." The fight was on and the nun almost lost her habit. She freaked and I got roughed up right there in front of my classmates and I never shed a tear. I thought, "fuck her I will never cry again to satisfy these stinky bitches."

One thing I do remember is that those nuns did stink badly. As she was roughing me up I thought to myself, "I wish I could kill her." I don't think I ever prayed again. I had no idea why this was happening. Apparently she did not like my prayer; go figure. Apparently I had defied the Lord or some shit like that. Anyway it seemed like I was always on my knees. If someone was not trying to stick their dick in me or my mouth or mauling me, I was praying, and I never knew what the fuck I was praying for. I just did what I was told. I lived in a constant fear of my surroundings. I became very good at hiding my feelings and I quit crying. I was a good con even at the age of six. I had no choice but to learn these tactics. It was for my own survival. It was do or die. I was so young, yet so wise.

I lived in this place for nearly a year and it was hell, well to me it was hell. The nuns were mean and damn grouchy bitches. They systematically demeaned me; mostly due to the fact I was an Indian. Although I did not have any recollection of what being Indian was I was hated because I had brown skin, go figure. They tried so hard to assimilate me. They tried to make me into something I was not. They were just as messed up as I was, if not worse. The difference was they were calculative! Everything that I became and everything that happened to me had an impact on the way I would live out my days. It was the way it was supposed to be at the time and at the place. I remember I could not learn in those classrooms. I'm not saying the lil white kids were not beaten, but I remember always being strapped. It is what is. Anyway, I remember my moms came to visit me once and I thought I was in heaven. Apparently she had gone somewhere with her new man. I was so happy to see her and I figured she was coming to rescue me. There she was sitting right in front of me. I could see her. I could touch her. I could smell her. She was right there within my grasp, then, just like that she was gone. Again I was totally crushed and I cried like I have never cried before. I tried not to cry but in this case I cried like Niagara Falls. I was so sick in my heart it was not even funny. After she was gone the nun gave me a beating because she said I should not cry. She said I was lucky to have a mom because some of these poor little kids had nothing. They were orphans. The package my mommy brought me would never be mine. I had no idea what an orphan was either and I couldn't have given a shit really. I mean I was not really an orphan because I had living parents; they just did not live together is all. Fact, my parents split up, no one wanted me so here I was. I was here because I was a non-Status Indian with no place to call home. So I lay in my bed and there I cried myself to sleep thinking of my beautiful mommy. I felt so broken, so lost and so lonely. I wished I could die but I did not know how to commit suicide, not yet. The nun told me I should be grateful God spared me. Yeah! God was a fucking hero all right; a regular Boy Scout. He had done right by me all right. You got to remember I had no belief in God at this time, I mean I was only six years old, what did I know? So there I would stay and put up with daily abuse. The only thing that did stop was the sexual abuse. Sadly, they were there waiting, festering in their sick skins, just waiting until they could get their hands on me once again.

    My family was my life but we were broken apart over the years that would follow. I never really had a life or a childhood to speak of. I lived strictly in an adult world. I try remembering some good times but it is difficult. This is reality. The best times in my life were with my mom and dad even though they were separated. We may have lived in desperation but I know that I was loved and loved dearly. They attempted at a marriage that failed. If they would have stayed on Sakimay perhaps things would have been different, but we will never know now will we? All I know is their lives were messed up, as mine would become. I am sure they only wanted the best for us but they did not know how to achieve their goals. I mean my parents must have had goals because we all do in some way or another. If they had dreams I am not sure what they were. I do know that we lived only in the moment nothing more, nothing less. You see I come from a long line of alcoholics, drug addicts, working girls, and street people. I do not know too many of my people who were not involved in the street life in some manner. Life was very dull yet exciting. But to top all of this it would become a very lonely place for me to be. There would be abuse that conquered all!

You know at the end of the day it was just that no one explained to my pops he should not abuse his wife or his children. Sadly in the days gone by you were essentially on your own at the mercy of the world around you. So people had no choice but to go through life un-counseled and suffered the undying wrath of alcohol and drugs. For that matter Indian people were not even recognized as human until the late 50's or into the 60's, but that is news for another book. Besides, that topic has already been extensively researched so we will leave it alone. What could one do with no help? Not much really. They had to live in a world that hated them because they were not white. That is the way life was and still is today. When I think back now I can recognize all the symptoms and problem areas my family faced. No one talked about shit. It was merely swept under the rug and that is it where it stayed. Feeling after feeling was left undealt with and buried deep in our souls. It is not that no one cared; it's just that no one knew how the hell to get it together and keep it that way. Slowly, effortlessly, and painfully our lives were shattered and ripped to shreds, person by person, and there was no one to stop the destruction that would take hold. It all seemed so hopeless. There did not seem to be an end to crisis after crisis. The years became cold as steel, as did my life.

Living as I lived was extreme. I had nowhere to go and nowhere to hide from what was going to happen. I had no idea how to stop the abuse that would penetrate my inner being and take away the child within. From what happened to me there was born a twisted unloving woman. The fear in my heart and soul were untouchable. As I reminisce my days on this earth I wonder why we stay so confused. Over the years I have figured this out. I was left alone to fend for myself and I did not do such a good job. I lived fast, far too fast, and it only brought me great amounts of stress, grief and hardship. I thought everything I was doing was right. I had no idea not really. I let people take away my dignity, my serenity, and my childhood. Furthermore, they took away all that I had as a child and left an empty hardened shell of a human. The sexual abuse would be devastating to my existence – but I survived.

Sexual Abuse: The Suffering of a Child
My earliest recollection of sexual abuse was at the age of three. I remember there were lots of people around and it might have been at a party; there were always lots of parties and such. I remember lying on

the floor in a bedroom on a mattress. The bedroom was at the back of the house off the kitchen. I'm not sure if I had bloomers on or a diaper, but I remember my uncle lay down beside me and stuck his hand in my bloomers or diaper. I remember feeling so afraid, and because of that fear, I never said anything. I am not even sure I would have had enough words at three years of age to express my pain and fear in that moment. I know I didn't like how his hand felt, and I attempted to move, but he held me firm, and then my memories are gone just like that. I do know that every time I seen him thereafter I was afraid and I would do my best to stay out of his reach. My next memories come from when I was around five years of age.

Later on in my sobriety my memories came back tenfold, and I very clearly remembered the sexual abuse. Those would be the years that would make me the woman I turned out to be. The arrow would pierce my heart and hold fast. The sexual abuse took hold and it destroyed my very being. My life would become scrambled like six eggs. It was three of my uncles who would pollute my soul, and my child spirit would be damaged. I could almost see her leaving, and she would run away and hide for years to come. It was a horrible thing for a small child to have to go through.

I don't remember the very first time, but I do remember the many times. My uncle would have me sitting on his knee, pretending to be the doting uncle, and meanwhile he had his shriveled up old dick out of his pants rubbing it against my skin or on my vagina, as he would push my panties over; the sick fuck. It doesn't matter how many times I talk or write about this, it still puts a big lump in my throat. You know he was supposed to love me like a niece, but instead he treated me like a whore. He was really violent and would be extremely aggressive. He took chances too, and even if there were people around he always had his gross disgusting smelly fucking hands on me. One time he had me in his room with my pants to the ground, and he was lying on top of me rubbing my vagina, and I would feel something warm and sticky run down my ass. It was fucked up. I remember he would be rubbing me, and I would get these warm feelings that actually in all honesty felt good, but when it was over I felt fucking dirty. I just wanted to die. I guess you would call them orgasms if you were a woman, but I was a mere child. Or he would have me sitting on his knee with his old stank penis stuck between my legs and he would move ever so lightly so no one knew what he was doing and he fucking got away with it. I would try to move away, but he held me tight until he was finished. What a sick fuck. It never took long but to me, as a child, it was a whole lifetime. I wanted to die. I just wanted to die.

I just wanted to fall into a hole and stay there. I tried to stay away from him, but the money he gave me kept me at his disposal. Yes that is correct, he gave me money. And being a kid well I loved candy, I mean what kid doesn't dig candy? The darkness crept in like a thief in the night. My soul would close itself to the world, and I would lay in that darkness and wish for death. Now you tell me what the fuck a five year-old kid knows about death. Time and time again the abuse went on and on and on. I remember at one point I would go to him because he had by this time conditioned me. I had money coming in, and those little orgasms were kind of cool for a minute. I would go to him and sit close or on his knee, and he would do his business. I do remember trying to stop it, but he told me if I told anyone he would hurt me or someone in my family. It was like living in a perpetual fucking nightmare that just went on forever. It was like watching your life disappear right before your own eyes. I was just screwed to the core.

    There was a shed outside my kokum's (grandmother's) house in the back by the outhouse. It was dark, damp, and smelled of mold. You know, I am afraid of the dark and could never understand why until I remembered my life, and when that happened it all came to light, it all made sense. I finally would figure out where that fear was ignited. He put an arrow in my heart. Anyway, he would take me to this shed, or after being conditioned I would go meet him there, and we would do our business in the icy-cold dark of that horrible little shed. The windows were all blacked out so it was the perfect haven for a fucked up old child molester. I remember every feeling, every moment of remorse that he bestowed on my soul, and it was absolutely gruesome. What he did to me would be devastating; he took away my child's spirit and my breath. I was his whore to have and to hold. As long as that money kept coming, so did I, so to speak.

    I was a little girl without a soul. Little girls should be playing in the mud. Little girls should be playing with dolls and should be just enjoying life. Little girls should be running free and living safe. Little girls should be playing in the snow making angels. Little girls should feel safe wearing cute little dresses. Little girls should be trying out their mommy's makeup and playing dress-up. Little girls should be playing with their moms shoes and stuff. Little girls were not supposed to know what I knew or what I experienced. Me, well, I was feeling penises. I was touching them, and I would feel them on my ass or near my vagina. I would know what a penis tasted like. What the fuck was he thinking? Where had his life gone so wrong that he had to fuck so deliberately with mine? Had he been abused as a kid or what? I have no idea, all I know is I would allow him to sexually abuse me for years, what seemed like fucking bazillions of years. Everyday for years I would be victimized, raped, and abused—morally, emotionally, physically, mentally, and verbally. I was a train wreck going nowhere fast. I grew to care very little about men except my dad and my brothers.

Arrow in my Heart

They would be the only men I ever truly loved without remorse or regret. I was so ashamed, so demoralized, so victimized and I had nowhere to run and nowhere to hide. I was broken.

I remember being repulsed by the look and feel of his old shriveled up penis. I could not understand what he was doing and why it looked the way it did and it was stinky too, real gross. And after a session when he was done he would ejaculate all over my ass, or my stomach or my legs all the while continuing to touch me till he was finished. Sometimes he would make me put his penis in my mouth. I should have bit it off now that I think of it, the old bastard. He was violent and he got off on it. The horror of that time in my life enveloped me and put me in a state of perpetual fear and it would follow me many years. Sometimes we would almost get caught but we didn't, and really I think we did but my memory is sketchy. I remember someone getting mad at me. I wanted to get caught. I wanted it to stop and I think he sensed it. He told me not to tell anyone or he might hurt my mom. He told me it was our secret. It was just so fucked up and so unreal. He said he loved me and that I was his little girl. The sick fuck. I know today he could have not done shit to me or to anyone else. But at five or six years of age I didn't know that and I was afraid and I kept my mouth shut. Day after day I lived with his abuse. He would wet my vagina with his tongue or his fingers and do what he did best the old fuck. In that shed if he heard someone coming he would put his hand over my mouth. He told me to shut-up or else. I was drawn into this darkness and I was at his disposal. I hated him with every fiber in my body and if I could have killed him... in a fucking heartbeat you best believe that right there. I woulda shot him in his black heart and cut off his dick and shoved it up his ass!! My *kokum's* house would be my coffin. I was unhappy. I was lost. But no one saw it. They all had their own issues to contend with. I mean I think they didn't see it or didn't know and to be honest I am not even sure, but what I am sure of is that I was sexually molested. That is the truth. I know in my heart there is no way that I could have been the only kid this old fuck was abusing, no way in hell. I remember there were lots of kids around, so he must have had a smorgasbord of kids to fondle and abuse. I remember living in fear all the time. I hated going to my *kokum's* house. I just remember this so vividly and at first I figured that people wouldn't believe me until I was older and learned about the Residential School system. Then I knew yes I would be believed. This wasn't a dream or a movie. This was my reality. Did I tell ya he paid me? Yeah, well he did and I bought candy; it kept me quiet.

There was another uncle in the States who would have his way with me. What the fuck was wrong with these men? I was a niece for God's sake, or was there a God, I think not. How could He let this happen to a child? How could He just watch while a child was been sexually violated? I would figure this all out later. This round of abuse would not last too long. My uncle would only have a few bouts with me and then it would be over. I only lived in Montana for a short time with my dad and brother's. This one would attempt to penetrate me but he could not really get it up; just like the last one. He couldn't have penetrated a fucking marshmallow. I wish I would have known what his purpose was but I never did figure it out. I cannot remember how many times he abused me but it was a few for sure. Every time we were alone in his trailer events took place. We had been living on a farm in really rural Montana, and for him this was perfect. We were totally isolated. I just hated being alone with him, and I would beg my dad to take me with him whenever he was about to leave, but sometimes he had to work or do something where I had to stay back. My uncle would wait for a while until he knew the coast was clear and then he would call me and I knew it was time. He would do disgusting things to me and I wanted death to open its doors and let me in. He would crawl on top of me and pump hard. It would hurt and I would cry. I was so afraid, so afraid, and no one was there to help the child within. He would have me straddled on his knee and he would be licking me and sticking his finger in my vagina. I was so sick in my soul, so very sick. Money it was always there and I always had my hand out. The dead Presidents were my friends, my only friends.

 I was mortified to no end. I remember one time he had me on the bed in the back of the trailer and he had his pants off as well as mine. He was trying to kiss me, he was touching me and he was making terrible noises. I was crying and he told me to shut-up and he hit me. He just kept touching, rubbing and trying to put his dick inside of me. I could feel it. I kept crying but only silently. I was so confused and so lost in this sexual abuse that I encountered over and over. I did not know what was up or down and I did not know what I could do to get out. The paint was peeling and peeling fast. My life was fucked but good. Why was this happening? Why is there no one around to save my little life? Why? Why? Why? That is all I could think of. I did not understand how a grown man, or men, who were family could do these fucked up things to me. This bastard use to send me to the neighbors to get fucked by an old man that lived there too. My uncle in essence was my pimp. As I said there was always money involved and I took it. I did what I did to survive the madness. I took what I took in order to comfort the deadness that lived in my mind, body and soul. I was mesmerized. The money took hold and never let go, money was truly the root of all evil and the men who dished it out. These men made me the monster I would become. I never had a chance. From this time on I would become very reckless in all my endeavors. These men, these pigs, all defied me as a child. The dirty rotten fucking pricks. They did not treat me as if I was a worthy niece or a family member, but rather they treated me like the whore I would become. If I could have ripped out their black hearts through their assholes you best believe that I would have in a fucking heartbeat. They stole my child. They stole my innocence as a baby. They killed me. Each and every time these creatures of the darkness touched me a small part of me diminished to never come back, until this moment in this time at the present. I have had to struggle every day of my life to accept what they did to me and I finally have at long last. For this I owe God my life. I cannot even begin to explain what this did to me. The arrow pierced my heart.

I was robbed. I was robbed of my childhood and of my youth and I had no idea the sexual abuse was wrong. I mean at such a young age it was difficult to decipher the rights and wrongs of the world. I have hated my uncle's all of my life and could never pray for them and if I did I would pray for horrible things to happen to them. Actually, in all reality, I still do not pray for them. I have wished so many bad things on them but I had to do it in order for me to maintain my bridges to sanity. I would have tortured them mercilessly without compassion, thought or conscious. I know that you cannot fight violence with violence or fire with fire but that is what they did to me. They made me into an ugly person that I would hate even more than I hated them. The sad thing is that I had made a pact with the devil/God that every man that came into my life would feel my wrath because of what my Uncles did to me. All I know is now, today – at this moment – in this time – I can honestly say – good-bye! I was sexually violated and raped as a child, however I am still alive. I have made it through with the help of my Creator with a power greater than myself and yes I have survived.

As horrifying as it was I understand today that sexual abuse is not acceptable nor is it to ever be tolerated. When I look back at my life, at what happened to me as a child, I finally understand that none of it was my fault. Had I not walked with God I would have surely perished. Back in the day people were ignorant to a lot of things until we discovered that we had a choice. Life is too short to hold the past. At some point you have to give it up to heal and I have been healed thus far.

I realize our lives are only lent to us. Therefore we must live it to the fullest. The suffering is over. I am no longer a victim. I am able to make my own choices. I am the one who holds my own destiny. No one can ever make me do things that I do not want to do, not now, not ever. But, the sexual abuse certainly did wreak havoc on my poor life. I did shit just for the sake of doing it. I just did what I did because I had to. I did shit without remorse, or care, or rhyme nor reason or compassion. I never needed a reason. I merely took it upon myself to do whatever I figured had to be done.

I am worth more then what I have suffered. I know this today. It has taken me a lifetime to figure shit out, but at least I did. Yes, I suffered as a child, but I have also excelled as an adult. My life at long last is safe. God has granted me the Serenity to accept the things that I cannot change, the Courage to change the things that I can and the Wisdom to know the difference. Is that not the truth?

I have been taught that it is extremely important to forgive and let go. Otherwise you might not totally heal. You see all these years I figured I was good and that I didn't have to forgive my uncles, so part of me stayed in a dark place. When I would hear about sexual abuse or read about it the first things that came into my head were my uncles and I could feel myself getting mad. There were times I even cried about it and lashed out negatively. If I was healed this would have not bothered me, so I had a decision to make. Do I forgive them? Honestly, yes I do. For a very long time I was content to hate them, but then I heard an Elder speak of forgiveness and about how we cannot move on if we do not forgive. She said we would stay stuck hating, resenting and never growing. So, yes I forgive my uncles for what they did to me as a child. It no longer cuts like a knife. I had to forgive. It is still a bit tender because it has only been in the last year that I finally forgave them but it's all-good, I got this.

CHAPTER 3

Years Into The Darkness

Years Into The Darkness

*M*y life was in and out of darkness. My dark passenger would stay with me for years. Speaking with my grandchildren recently made me realize that I do not remember any Christmases or Easters or All Hallows' Eves or Valentine's Days or any of those special little holidays that they love so much. I do not really remember getting presents or candy or stuffed animals, but I surely remember being violated and raped. I don't remember the Tooth Fairy leaving me money under my pillow, but I remember being paid like a prostitute. I don't remember searching for Easter Eggs that the Easter Bunny left, but I remember my soul being taken as a child. You know maybe that is why I am not really hip on celebrating those holidays because mine were never any good.

By the time I was fifteen years old I was using intravenous drugs, and by the time I was seventeen years old I was a full-fledged alcoholic with a severe drug problem. I had no idea what I was doing, and my moms just did the best she could with what she had. Her life was miserable, something I did not understand until I went through hell, grew-up, and sobered up. Once my memories kicked in I knew she had a rough life, but she is gone now, and it's not my story to tell—just know that she suffered, and suffered hard. I do love her, and I have missed her every day of my sad fucked up life; she was my gold and she was taken away from me when she was way too young. So anyway, my life goes awry. I stumble, I fall, and sometimes I do not get up because I am beat. I wanted to die and I would attempt to take my own life a few times, but I think I was actually looking for pity rather than death. I was so lost. School was not easy either.

I had a difficult time with school and this is because I was bounced from one school to another. I did not fare well. I did Grades 5 or 6 to 8 at Regent Park School. I must have been at about four schools prior to this. I am not saying that this happens to all kids; however, it did not do me any justice that is for sure. Because I had no structure I would fail miserably at school even though I must say I did try. Listen for a moment. If you are wise let your children stay in one school. It will make their lives and yours more livable. Don't let your kids be losers. Let them have a chance at a decent education. I mean that is not to say all kids will end up buttheads, however guaranteed the majority will. Trust me it is just better for a child to focus on one school rather than four or five or even six. It is much easier to learn and to have discipline. I am talking from experience. Listen and learn. It may save a child from what I have been through.

I was always in trouble and it was rare that I ever listened to what was being taught; I dragged those teachers through hell and back. I never understood anything in school especially math. No one took the time to help the poor little Indian. The teachers put most of their focus

An Arrow In My Heart

on those who excelled and I was not one of those types; but I could have been. I was put on the back burner burned to a crisp. You cannot really blame anyone because back in the day no one knew how to care and I was trip to say the least. I would skip school to go meet my boyfriend. His name was Jonnie and he was a fly looking white guy. He never tried to have sex with me and he was very sweet. We spent as much time together as we could. I was fourteen and he might have been eighteen or so. He wasn't very tall. He made me feel like a princess. I don't even know how I met him. I had a group of buddies that were badass and they were white kids and they got away with a lot being white and all; it was a given. All of a sudden I meet him and fall madly love. I was in heaven being with him. I felt so loved and so important. He was my first crush. He made me feel so grown up when I was with him. When I close my eyez I can picture him. Good times, good times. All his attention was always on me. He would roll up to my school too to see me and dayum that was hot; an older boy. Well I was like strutting around like I was something. One day I was visiting my families graves a few years ago in Regina and low-n-behold I found his grave marker. I am not sure how long we were together, but I would slither on because this guy wasn't giving me what I wanted. And he may well have dumped me, who knows? All I know is he was good for my ego. He stroked it. Back to school.

The principle was one of my teachers and I drove him nuts and almost into seclusion. I heard through the grapevine that he was an alcoholic. I wonder if I had anything to do with his addiction or did I simply add stress to his addiction? I remember I use to get him so angry that he would turn beet red and one vein on his forehead would stand out. I just stood by and waited for it to pop. I loved this shit and I would do things on purpose just to see him rattle. I seemed to be in his office or the hallway all the time. In those days we still got the strap and damn that thing would hurt. He would hit my hands as hard as he could and I would just look at him and smile. It made him furious to say the least. He wanted me to cry but I never did. Never shed a tear. I refused to give him the satisfaction. I would look at him and think fuck no, ain't no man every going to hurt me again. Ever! My uncles did a lot of damage to say the least. But, when I was alone the tears would come. I could not let him see this though. I had to show him I was strong and that nothing hurt. At thirteen I was very good at hiding my feelings. You never showed your weakness. It was a learned behavior; remember? I had nothing to lose. I was hoping one day his blasted head would pop from being so angry with me.

I remember this one time there was this kid who was

always bugging me. He would pull my braids and just do dumb shit. I told him to back off and leave me alone. Of course I had started my 'time' (read: periods) and my moms didn't tell me how it was gonna be or feel. I learned all on my own. Anyway, back to this assneck. I warned him. Everyday there was always something. He would move my desk, take my stuff, put shit on my seat and just be annoying. I played football and he would try tackling me, muhtay it was Tag Football but he was a little pervert. He was very constant I must say. He would hide my shit around the class. He was always groping at my boobs and I would slap his hands away. Slap me on my ass. But one day, oh yes one day, I came to school in a bad mood and he was like a lil dog jumping around. I ignored him for the better part of the day. It was nearing the end of the day and I was tired. He did something and I just attacked him and pulled Ninja on his ass. And then I saw red. I grabbed him and slung him to the floor. I was kicking, punching and I picked him up by the collar and threw him into the lockers at the back of the room. At one point I had him in a full-nelson on the floor and I think he was screaming like the bitch he was, but I am not sure. I know he was making some kind of choking sound. The whole time I was doing this I was crying and screaming telling him that he should have just left me the fuck alone. I was throwing his ass all over that classroom. Over desks, against the chalkboard, you name it his ass seen and/or felt it. And, no one came near. Everyone backed way up. I must have traumatized those poor little white kids because they all scattered. Finally the Calvary comes to rescue his ass and guess who got in trouble. Yes, that is correct, I was expelled for three days and would get the strap; but I sure did kick the shit outta that lil bitch. Man I never felt so powerful by beating the skin off some lil douche bag; best end to a day ever. I did see him when I got back to school and he was still busted up, but I tell you that he never fucked with me again. He learned that I was a weapon not to be reckoned with. He stayed away from me, forever! He was a trip.

    This insanity in my life carried on. Yes my moms settled in life but I was too far-gone for anything else. Whether or not she knew anything of the street life I really don't know. I mean my brother, my sister, my cousins, my uncles, my aunts were we all Street people and if she knew well she never spoke of it. My dreams would be not. My hopes and aspirations were not. I would follow what would have to be my destiny. I know that I had to go through what I did in life to get here to this point. I am blessed. The Street would call me...

The Arrow in my Heart: My Descent into a Life of Drugs, Alcohol, and Prostitution

I turned my first trick when I was eighteen years old. I would hit the street right after my moms passed away and my child had been taken away from me, so I had fuck all to lose; I'd lost it all already! And I am not talking about my inner child but rather my baby that I had at the age of seventeen. You see, prior to that I was a very good thief, and I could steal anything that you wanted. As long as it was not nailed down I would get it. That was my job: I would steal for the older hookers that were on the street, some of them were family and friends of the family. We all fit into the same mold and had the same lives. I was the girl and grew to believe that I was indeed important. I would take orders for clothing, and away I would  go. And I must say it was a might bit lucrative. I would go out as soon as the stores would open with my list and bring all the goods back to the bars where the lovely women hung out. It felt so good. I felt so powerful not getting caught. I wasn't doing a whole lot of dope but it was there lingering waiting in the dark for me to come to it and I would. I loved being high. It gave me a sense of relief and peace of heart. I made good money back then, but I started to get sloppy. Oh, and I would charge up drugs and stuff—my money from boosting would pay for that—but I started doing more drugs and owing more money. I could not always foot the bill so one of the older girls took me to the side and said that I better pay my bills or else. So at eighteen I turned that first trick and it would be so disgustingly devastating, but it was all I knew. And so my life of prostitution would be born.

After that first one the drug addiction kicked in and kicked in hard because I could not stand what I was doing. All the memories I had locked in my head about the sexual abuse my uncles bestowed upon me came flooding out, and it was like a fucking tornado attacked me. The drugs took away the pain and the memories. So I became a working girl, a child of the night. I was a stalker of men's money to keep me supplied in drugs and alcohol. Yes, a vixen. I would doll up accordingly, put on a pound of makeup, wear six-inch stilettos, short skirts, and I would roam the streets like a vampire looking for blood. I would sell my wears in Saskatchewan, British Columbia, and Manitoba. It was a lucrative business if you were not a hardcore drug addict, and if a person was smart they could save, but I was not that person. I spent it as fast as I made it. I never really had a pimp; I mean I had men I would give money to because I loved them—NOT. The men I had, well, they were nothing. Just a piece of ass that I would give money to because that was what a hooker was supposed to do: she was supposed to love and support her man.

I was introduced to Sista' Heroin, and oh my God I thought I struck fucking gold. The shit was that good. I remember the first time I did it; I was in Calgary with my aunt and uncle. I was nineteen or twenty years of age. I went there with my dad; it was after my brother was shot—we will talk about that later. My uncle was a drug dealer, and in those days he dealt some of the best heroin money could buy. It was pure gold. I remember watching him prepare a fix for me. He opened up a little cap of stuff that looked like salt and pepper. He put it in a spoon, added water, heated it up, and sucked it back up into a syringe. I was feeling very afraid and not sure what to do, but I just watched with great anticipation. He put a tie around the top of my arm and made me pump it, and my virgin veins popped like a bride's cherry on her wedding night. He tapped my vein and stuck in the needle, and drew it back. The blood seeped into the syringe, then he slid the plunger in, and that is all I remember.

I do vaguely remember feeling like I was floating and that my head felt so strange. It was like I had an out-of-body experience. Fuck I was so stoned. I woke up in a bathtub full of cold water. My uncle and aunt were kneeling down and talking to me, but it was all foggy. My dad leaning over was asking why his baby was in the bathtub with all her clothes on, but I cannot remember what my uncle said. All I know was that I was experiencing the highest high I would ever have in my entire life. I felt like I was on fire. I felt like I could walk on fucking water, that is how stoned I was. Apparently, my uncle gave me the whole cap when I should have only had half of it, and damn I was fried. I remember changing my clothes and shit it took a long time. I remember that next I was standing up, and I was on the nod against the wall. I was trying really hard to wake up, but I did not really want to. I wanted to feel what I was feeling right there and I never wanted to wake up from that. I could have just stayed like that forever. It was fucking awesome. I could hear my uncle talking, but it was like he was talking in a tunnel. He told my aunt that I'd better go for a walk so I would not go under again. They were worried that I might overdose again. That shit was good.

So he sent me to the store that was, oh, maybe a block away from his house. I remember walking, but it was like in slow motion. And when I waved my hand in front of my face it was like it was following, you know like a bunch of hands slowly going after the first one. I felt like I was a hologram. I could not believe how stoned I was and how great I felt all at the same time. Fuck, I was in heaven: heroin would become my friend and my lover. I walked to the store, and it took me at least an hour or so just to go there and back. I would come to, and I would be on the nod standing up or leaning against a wall or a fence. I am not sure what happened after, but I know I would do more heroin, this most voluptuous drug, with my uncle. But I would not do as much. My life lay in every cap of heroin, or any other drug or alcohol I would consume in my life. My life would stay stuck in a world where I would never be satisfied. There is more to come.

Let's back up for a moment at my first fix. I was fifteen. As I stated I had some shady friends that were drug dealers and/or knew drug dealers. I was in someone's basement and they were fixing Tuinals (a nerve or sleeping pill) but it gave ya a good kick. It was my turn. So again I watched my friend/kinda boyfriend, he had drugs. I was watching him get the stuff ready. He put it in a spoon, cooked it and sucked it back up in a syringe. Tied my arm off and sent it home. We were in the bathroom and he asked me if I felt anything and I said no. He told me to stand up, so I stood up and that's all I remember. Down for the count, I came to and I was on the couch and holy shit I was blasted. I could barely move. I felt like a rag doll. When I tried to get up I'd fall over. It took a while but eventually I got it together and did more. I didn't really like this stuff but it was there so I did it. You now that first high? That is why people get so addicted. They want to have that feeling. It's called *Chasing the Dragon*! But you will never get that first high affect ever again... it's gone, hence: Addiction. Raw and rough, never easy!!

I remember one time back in the day and a few of us decided to go to Winnipeg. One of my buddies knew some cool drug dealer type people there so off we went. It was Woodstock time and it had just been put on the big screen. So we all got shit faced stoned on LSD and went to the drive-in and damn it was just almost like being at the actual Woodstock. It was bloody hell awesome. We partied with these dudes after and I remember being so stoned. One of them took a fancy to me; he had drugs of course, so I would be his for the weekend. It was just crazy at how high we all got and no one went under. It was mostly drugs with some alcohol but who wanted to fuckup a perfectly good high with too much booze. We stayed there for the weekend and I made my mark in Winnipeg with this fine, fine young man, nudge, nudge, wink, wink. Young and very dumb indeed.

We lived on the edge constantly. It was all or nothing. I remember one time we drove from Regina to Saskatoon and I had a big ass cast on my leg but nothing held me back ever, not even a broken body part. I remember the driver was flying, it's amazing we just didn't all crash and die. We got to Saskatoon *semak* (Cree for right away) and off to the bar we went. I lost my crutch somewhere along the way so my cousin just carried me into the bar over his shoulder. Always an adventure to say the least. Party's, drinking, drugs and men were the only things on my life menu and not necessarily in that order. It just was. I remember going to booze cans after the bars closed, now that was a blast. The booze was a lil cheaper and there of course were drugs to be had. Life was interesting to say the least.

CHAPTER 4

More Rigorous Adventures Of My Life On The Street

So where do I go from here? There is so much to share and talk about to give you a really good understanding of exactly why my life got so messed up. Let's just talk. Okay, so I hit the street and was introduced to prostitution at the age of eighteen. Now remember, by this time, I am pretty much fucked from the years of sexual abuse. I hung around in skid row bars in Regina, Calgary, Winnipeg, Vancouver, and even in little old Prince Albert. Yeah, that was the life—nowhere to go and nowhere to hide. One day was the same as the next. There were a few times where I would actually have a little job in skid row bars in Regina when I was pretending to be normal, whatever that was. I was underage too, so don't ask me how I worked, but I did. My pay was under the table, so I never paid my taxes. In a couple of the bars I also had a trick room so when one of my regulars came in, I could take a coffee break, go make a few bucks, and hit the floor selling beer after I was done. For you laymen out there, a trick room is a room specifically for having quick sex for money, and a trick is the man who pays for the sexual services of his liking.

Yes, I thought I had it all: I was the girl, I was invincible, and no one could hold a candle to my ass. I was perfect. Men—and even some women—wanted me, but I never did a woman. I just could not do that since it was against my morals—yeah, like I had any. I just wasn't into women. I was a class act. I had sex for money, how classy was that? But I did not know any better; it was just life. You remember, I was on this mission to pay back all the men in my life—well, prostitution was a perfect place to be and do just that. Payback was a bitch. I could be as violent and kinky as I wanted to be. I could beat men, piss on them, shit on them, and they paid me good money. Yep, it was the life. Like I said, the odd time I would have a man who I would give money to, but it was all just for show. I mean I did secretly want someone to love me for who I was, even though I was very little at the time. I had seen lots of relationships where women appeared happy, and that is what I wanted; I did not know they too were dying in silence as we all lived our lives in hell. You know, if you cannot love yourself who the hell else are you going to love?

I fought myself every step of the way. I climbed up the ladder of success in the criminal world, and I would become important, but not to myself. I thought I was pretty hot shit and that I was very bad. If I saw a man I wanted, and he already had a woman, I would take him even if it meant breaking up a family. If the guy was stupid enough to follow me, so be it. I would use him, and he would use me. Fair was fair. I looked at it as a win/lose situation and it was win for me and lose for whatever dude I was with. I even had men tell me they loved me. I was desirable. I was wanted but never needed. I was had but never loved. Even my husband had belonged to another. His woman was my friend, and we had a fight that led me to be so angry that I just took her man—and married him. If I saw anything I wanted, I just took it. That was how I rolled. Men were a dime a dozen, and even if it was some other bitch's sloppy seconds, so be it, I would make it mine. However, somewhere in the insanity I did fall in love with my husband before he would die of an overdose, but he would never know. It was always too late in my world, just always too late. The arrow would pierce my heart long and deep.

My Family Affairs
You know we had moments of clarity where my husband and I would both not be high and talk about the future; it was so sad. Or we would just smoke dope and be mellow, and then we would love and talk about life. I am not even sure what year I married him but the day was April 12th and I know it was in the 70's. I remember that my cousin decided I needed a before I get married party and so we proceeded to get high and drunk. My husband-to-be came by the room to see me, but my friends told him to hit the road—that he could not see me till the next day at the court house where were married by a Justice of the Peace. I guess he got mad. All he wanted to do was see me. The next day we start rolling and I am still half drunk and my husband-to-be was nowhere to be found. Not sure what happened but he was found and we were married. The party after was nuts of course; why wouldn't it be? We were at his uncle's place and they had more booze then you can imagine. I remember falling down the stairs in my dress, not once but twice. It was just a joke. Our marriage was crazy. We had good moments but very few. I remember one time I tried to hang myself in a closet because I was mad at him. Thank goodness it didn't work. He would cheat on me, I would cheat on him—but we always ended up back together. A marriage not made in heaven for sure. We lived in hotels, motels and he did attempt to get me to stop turning tricks but it never lasted. I got along good with his people and they accepted me as I was, but we were destined to fail, like everything else in my life.

   I remember one time he was in the hospital in Regina. He got yellow jaundice. I came to town from Prince Albert and found out he was there so I went to visit him. He was so handsome. I can see him; I can almost feel him and it saddens me that I lost him. I wanted to be a good wife, but I didn't know how, and our marriage would fall apart like everything else in my life. He was not my destiny. That day I was with him in the hospital would be the last time I saw him alive. I looked at him and he was surprised to see me. He didn't say anything just smiled a weak sick smile. I closed the curtain, and I crawled into his bed with him, and we just lay there in each other's arms. It was nice for the moment. I do not know what we talked about, but I remember the moment. It was easy to be there and be with him. And I knew I fell in love with him at that very moment, but like I said he would never know the truth. He died of a drug overdose in 1983. That ends that.

My family was my life as was my husband; I just didn't know it till I cleaned up. Each of them would perish from one thing or another. My mom died when I was eighteen, my brother was shot when I was nineteen or twenty, my sister died when I was twenty-three or twenty-four, my dad would die when I was thirty, and my husband would die that same year. The loss of all these people who were so important to me would leave me to the vultures. I would float through life one day at a time just biding my time until I took my own life for real or until someone killed me. It was like living in a vacuum, always being sucked up and thrown around. My days were always the same, never changing. My brother, who was five years older than me, like I said, was shot and murdered. I remember this like it happened yesterday. Do not get me wrong, my siblings all have my love equally; however, this brother was closer to my age, and we had a good relationship. I hung around him more and we would cohabit. He did try save me from myself but I never listened to anyone but myself, and that didn't work so well for me. I need to speak of his death. His impact on my life has to be said, written about.

I had this bogus job at a place known as Native Youth. We were all street people trying to make life different for ourselves, but in essence we just had legal jobs where we could get high and party in the building after hours. I mean come on really like we knew what we were doing and the thing is we were trying to help others—not! We couldn't help shit if our mouths were full of it and we were full of it. This one day I was at work, and I got a phone call. The person on the other end told me that my brother had just been shot and was in the hospital.

I felt that darkness come over me again. I felt all the years of sexual abuse coming forth and pounding me to the ground. I felt my dark passenger creep into my soul. I could feel that arrow piercing deep into my heart. I didn't know what to do; I just sat there and looked at the phone. I think someone asked what was wrong and I said, "Joey just got shot". I was numb to the bone. I got to the General Hospital in Regina, and I think every street person in city was there. I remember seeing my dad, my uncles, my cousins, my enemies, his girlfriends of past and present. The police were there too. It was a regular gong show. People were holding each other and crying. I remember feeling like I was in a bubble. I felt like I was floating over everybody just looking down and wondering what the fuck just happened. I didn't know what to think. All I could hear was that he was shot; my brother was shot in the head. I thought, "What the fuck, no way I need to see him!" But they were not letting anyone in except my dad I think—it was very blurry. Police were taking the statements of those people he was in the bar with that day. Apparently, the shooter walked in the back door with a gun, past the bar, past the people, and just shot him in the head. I am not even sure what happened in the bar, it's all speculation and I don't want to speculate. All I know was that my brother was shot dead. I mean that kind of thing is only supposed to happen in the movies. This ain't supposed to happen in my world.

The chaos that surrounded my life at that moment was sheer insanity. My brother Joey lived an insane life. I remember he would try helping me with my math and get so mad because I couldn't get it. But he never gave up; he just kept on helping me. He was a very smart human when it came to school but he never made it. He could have been somebody that is for sure. I remember so many good things about him that I forget the bad. I know what he did was wrong, but when you love so deeply it's hard to see the wrong. He was abusive to his woman and would beat her ass. I grant you he should have not been violent, but that is his story to tell, and he is not here, so I won't go into this big long thing about him. All I know for sure is that he loved the children he had with this woman, but he would never get to know them. And it's not about talking shit about her now it's over and nothing will bring him back. I tell this story to share what this did to me, and the impact it had on my life.

I remember being in his hospital room and he had tubes all over the place. I felt numb. I was talking to him and telling him to come back. I told him I would give up my life and look after him forever. I begged him not to leave, and I think I was even praying. Well, it was more of a bargain with God, you know, "Take me not him" kind of thing. He had already passed away, but I didn't know that. I just stood by his side. I remember the bandages on his head, and one side of his face was so swollen he was almost unrecognizable. It was a deep, deep purple and black. I can actually feel that moment. I can feel the ache that I had in my heart so many years ago standing in that hospital room. I stood there and looked at him from head to toe. I noticed that his feet to his knees were cold, so I called for a nurse and requested blankets. The nurse knew he was dead but humored me and brought blankets. I covered his legs and I leaned over and held onto him like it was my life, he was my life. Oh my God this is hard even now, years later; I can feel my pain for his loss. I feel it right to my soul but its ok because I can handle it today. I will never forget how this makes me feel. I will hold it close. I don't ever want to forget what this did to me. I will teach that this is what violence, alcohol, drugs, and street life will do to you if you do not get out. It took my brother from me. They just kept putting that arrow in my heart life after life. He died! The others who passed on before me are also sadly missed. I pray to my mom, my dad, my sister, my husband, and to Junior because I loved them all so dearly. It is through them that I find the strength to carry on and live a good life. He would die at the tender young age of twenty-four.

My Sister
My sister passed on at the age of thirty-four I believe. All I can tell you is that she was awesome. This one time I was in the City Bucket waiting to go to jail and I had just fallen asleep. It was a Friday night. I wake up and there is a women yelling like a crazy bitch in the next cell. I'm yelling back telling her to shut the hell up and all of a sudden I recognize the voice, it was my sista! So I look through the hole in the wall and yes it was her. So now I'm trying to help the cops and settle her kettle. She is screaming and all kinds of shit. She was on the toilet and I realized that she was screaming because she had a miscarriage and the fetus was in her hands so now I start yelling for the cops who finally come. She settled when she recognized me and she was crying holding this little thing in her hands. This I will never forget, dayum. Anyway, the ambulance eventually came and took the fetus. The next time I seen her was at the Pine Grove Correctional Centre (The Grove); we ended up there together.

Man she was a funny woman. I think she was only with me for a couple of weeks, just long enough to dry out and clean up. I remember one day she called me to ask me to go grab the janitor as her toilet was plugged. So off I go to find him and I should have let the guard know too but oops I forgot. He gets his shit and goes to her cell and that crazy broad was sitting on her toilet buck nekid, dayum we laughed for days. You shudda seen the look on his face. It was priceless. He turned his self around and hauled ass outta there. We had a good time. She was telling me that I should stay outta jail you know just trynna be the older wiser sista. I loved her so. She always had her door open for me. I always had a place to crash. And really she was a good woman, just fucked up from the drugs and drinking. She never had a chance and the street would take her and have its way with her. Her story is not mine to tell but know this; if she had the chance I was given she too would have made it. But it was her destiny was to die, the Creator called her home.

The Eve's of Junior
Junior, the love of my life, was the second I truly loved. Yes, I'm using his name. This one was a forbidden love, and I am talking about it because, really, who is it going to hurt? And it is not meant to hurt it is a piece of my life I need to share. We had an understanding and that was that, nothing more nothing less. We never had a life together other than what there was, and it was true. We loved each other from

afar because he believed our family ties were too strong to break, and he had great respect for our family. I did too, but my love for him was stronger, and I would push him, and like a man he would falter and we would love each other nonetheless. But he would die, and again the arrow would pierce my heart and would be pushed back into the dark. He would call me on my birthdays, at Christmas, on Valentine's Day, at Easter... you name it he called. There would be times he would not even remember calling me because he was too high but he called. I remember this one time he did a store or something and had bags of money and cigarettes. I had just moved back from Prince Albert. He came to my place. He'd hurt himself, but had these bags of shit. He laid low healing for a few days and I asked him to marry me. He looked at me as if I was nuts and I did a futile attempt to talk him into it. But our family was in my way and he would not do it. Damn he was stubborn. I don't know what happened to the stuff he had and he was going to give me a bag but I pissed him off and he took it all. But he never stayed mad at me long. He gave me smokes and cash, but not his love the way I wanted it. We would meet at a family funeral or a family function and he would give me that "hey baby, I love you look forever" and he would look away. Or I would walk by him and touch his arm and smile. It was our lil game of love. Or I would lean into his ear and say something cheeky and he would just laugh. We had lots of great times together that I will hold in my heart forever. I just want to acknowledge the two most important men in my life who would not feel my wrath due to childhood sexual abuse. I would not go after them the way my uncles went after me. I would love them both in my own way. I will always love them.

In these years I would have two children that I would lose to family and the social welfare system. I was far too screwed up to have kids, but I never took any preventative measures for childbirth, and these children would be born into my insane life. I would try to parent them, but it didn't work for me. I had no idea how to care for them, or even how to love them. In order to love others you need to love yourself, and I surely did not. In fact I literally hated who I was and what I had become. But I had no idea how to get out, so my life slipped deeper and deeper into the abyss. My children would suffer, and I would suffer. I had another child when I was thirty, but this one I would hold onto with my life. I was still using, getting older but no wiser. To make a long story short, I would not lose her to anyone or

anywhere. She would also suffer the way the other two did, but I hung on. I know I was a bad parent, and I have come to terms with that. I was not prepared to be a mother, yet I would bring three children into my fucked up existence. I had so many things wrong in my life, and my poor children would meet my wrath. It is their stories to share if they wish. I just need to affirm that I indeed have three children whom I love dearly. That is a given. My children are still alive and I do not want to disclose too much because they have stories of their own. I mean yes I was a horrible mother, I know that but trust me I paid the piper and I paid fucking dearly for what I did to my children. I suffered my whole life and so I had to forgive myself for what I did to them and I have. It is now their turn to tell their story if they like and to forgive.

CHAPTER 5

Life In Jail: A World All It's Own

Life In Jail: A World All It's Own

From the time I was eighteen or nineteen, until I was thirty years of age, I was in and out of jail. I would think I was such hot shit because, you know, on the street if you went to jail that just meant you had made your mark. It was graduation time. I remember the first time I ever went to jail. I'd got caught for stealing. I remember my stealing days well; I would get high, go and try to steal, and I would get caught—which is another reason the prostitution kicked in. So anyway, I am in the RCMP cells waiting for transport to jail, and I was afraid. I had received a six-month sentence, and off I went to see the wizard. I was on this little plane with, oh maybe, thirty other inmates, mostly Indians and maybe a sprinkle of white folk for balance. The plane was hot and stinky because some of these men had not showered for days; it was ripe.

I remember we were on that plane all freaking day. They herded us off in shackles and handcuffs. I felt like such a villain. It was great really. I thought I was someone—but I was also afraid. So there I am in jail sitting in an office being interrogated then taken to be cleaned, debugged, checked for a venereal disease, and dropped into a cell that was maybe six feet by six feet with one window, a bed bolted to the floor, a cupboard, and a sink that was attached to a toilet. I remember acting tough, but when they closed that cell door it was a whole other ball game for sure. I cried like a baby, but no one would see. After that first sentence, and because I knew so many of the women inside, it got easier. You know I would have to say that going to jail actually saved my sorry ass because it would give me time to get my shit together and clean up. But as soon as I would get out I would run straight to the dealer man, and maybe get laid. It all depended on how messed up I would get, but drugs always came first.

I never really done any serious jail time, but then again I never got caught for everything very serious, and no I never killed anyone, close, but it never happened. I began my jail career in the early 70's, and the last time I was in would be in 1981. So for many years of my life I was in and out of jail. I think there was one year or so in there they missed me but I was in mostly every year. It was nothing but merely a rest for me. I think the longest stretch I did was about a year, give or take a few months. It was just a waste of time on the government's part, but the way I looked at it the money was not mine so who gave a fuck. As far as I was concerned it was coin well spent. The government was one big trick anyway. Am I right or what? You bet I am. Little did I know that the poor taxpayers had to dish out coin to keep my sorry ass in jail, but I never knew any better; nor did I care. So in essence my sorry ass was saved, go figure. I liked jail because I just felt tough being locked up. I had status. I was the girl. Remember now I was somebody. I met a lot of my street sisters in The Grove. Back in the day of incarceration I met some extremely dangerous women and I loved it. I wanted so much to be just like them. I wanted to be feared. I wanted to be noticed when I walked into a room. I wanted people to move when I walked by. I wanted all the power that I could possibly get. I mean I had some of what they had but I wanted more, I always wanted more. I wanted the Devil himself to bow to me. I wanted people to look up to me, to worship me. I wanted to be the most important woman around. I wanted to be dangerous. You know while I did become all these things and more, what I really became, when I'm honest, was a full-time loser, and, what is even sadder is that I became all these things only to myself. I was the enemy. I was my very own worst enemy and it all passed me by like two ships in the night.

I went to jail for stealing, breach of probation, parole violation, prostitution, assault, and so on. It was endless to what I did. I was always attempting to get away with stuff. I was always conning my way out of a bad situation. I did meet some pretty nice matrons (guards) while in jail. They treated us pretty good back in the day. Every once in a while a matron would come along who figured she had balls and would at- tempt to play the heavy, we always fixed them. I use to love those bitches because I was always a little tougher. I was never easily intimidated by anyone, especially a matron. The Grove was small and it made all the difference.

I did most of my time in a women's jail, which is up north in The Grove. It became my second home away from home. It became a place that I felt very comfortable in. I even felt safe if you can handle that. We were all the same, so it was easy to live in there. I remember I use to go to AA meetings with one of my cousins. She and I would meet up with a third cousin in the washroom and she would give me a mitt full of pills and being the pig I was I naturally would eat them all up. So when it came time for me to talk, you know it was all shit but it was all I knew so I went with it. Yeah I said I was an alcoholic but never admitting anything about drugs. I never really did understand anything about alcoholism either. I just said stuff because I thought I was supposed to. I do not know if my shit fooled anyone. I know my cousin who went straight was seriously hot at me because she had bumped hip and she was the one who got me out of jail for this meeting. But you know I never thought that for a moment I would have gotten her in trouble if I were found out. Although she knew she never said fuck all. As mad as she was she still loved me and encouraged me to be open at meetings. She never judged me ever. We still talk every once in a while. However, at the time her support would not help me because I was not ready to give in, not yet. I was not done fucking up my life or fucking up other people's lives. Nope, I was not done. No one could help me least of all her. I just did what I wanted, when I wanted, no holds barred, just did my own thing and moved on to the next whatever, or whoever whether it was animate or inanimate.

Another time we got some needle dope in and we went wild. It came to my turn and my friend gave me a powerful hit and boom I was down. The next thing I know I'm in my cell with my buddies at my side, I had gone under. The chance. The rush. The getting away with drugs in jail. The power, it was all I lived for. There was nothing better than pulling the wool over the guard's and it was so easy, they were easy. We could have gotten away with murder I am sure. No one cared. Life was good. It was proper. We were all at the peak of our lives and in jail. I never thought that I could have died right there in that jail cell. I am thankful my girls looked after me. I was okay and no one was any wiser about our trip. I would do more drugs later in jail.

Another time we were preparing for a Halloween dance. I had my friend's save me their drugs for better than two weeks. I was planning to party. In those days it was pretty easy to get drugs on the inside. It was their way of controlling us. Their way of soothing the savage beast within – here what I'm saying, yeah you know that. If they kept us subdued it was easier to live with us. I remember that I was on Valium and in those days they use to knock me out because I was not use to them. I took them four times a day and I was on my back for most of it. To be honest, I don't even know why I was on them but I got them so what the hell may as well enjoy the perks. Anyway back to the dance. In preparation of our costumes I had stolen most of the stuff from the craft room for both my girl and me. I was something I tell ya. Of course, I dressed up as a hooker. You know I always did this and I don't know why. Low self-esteem perhaps. It's that thing that if it is all of something that you know or you fit into it then do it. So anyway we all get costumed up and away we go. I had taken about thirty or forty pills. A variety was better. I was such a pill pig. I was severely tethered to say the least. I could not even stand straight, and I had the nerve to wear heels. I never did anything with caution. I was even dancing with the Director and did not remember. I wonder if I asked him to go out, you know to turn a trick. I was in the mood apparently. I was hamming it up at this dance and cannot remember too much. I would tell you all about it but I can't. I just remember getting ready, dancing once in a while, talking to people but that's pretty much it. The best part of all this was the staff had no idea about how fucked up I really was. I won yet again, or did I? My girl's looked after me because they said I was hanging around the staff too much and they did not want me to get busted so they kept me busy. You know that guard/inmate thang. I guess I was really being a heat score, but it was all a game, and no one really paid any attention in those days. As long as we did not cause any shit we were left alone. Besides you know back in the day we were all experts.

I even had a job once on the outside. I had been a good little inmate throughout my bit and toward the end I applied for Work Study or something or other and low-and-behold I landed a job; as did one of my cousins. Actually there were a few of us who scored this for the summer. I was going to be out in the fall, so I thought what the hell might as well not be broke whence I get out. It was a job in the field picking potatoes, carrots and shit like that. It was hot and we would be out all day. By the time we went back to jail we were all pretty tired. It was okay, it got us out for a whole day five days a week. Can't bitch about that, plus we were making a wage. Drug Money!! It was fun too because we fucked around a lot you know just passing time. I use to dig these big fat juicy earth worms out of the ground and chase my cousin around with them. Fuck these things were long, slimy and pink; got any memories – yah, ha, ha!! One of the lighter sides of being in jail.

I also did a few months in a joint in Vancouver called Oakalla. The processing was way rank. I was dope sick and in a bad mood as usual because I had gotten caught again on a fucking weekend. You know it was always on a damn weekend that my ass would get caught, dammit! Anyway, I'm in this room and there are matrons and other inmates all over the place. This one woman has me at her desk and she is asking me my history and shit, and I'm doing as I should. She looked at me and was quiet for a few seconds and says to me, "Are you queer?" I just looked at her and said shit because I was shocked at first. Then I said, "No are you"? She told me that she had to ask because they had a separate wing for the dikes, her words not nine, and she wanted to process me to the appropriate wing. So I figured okay that's cool I can handle this and I told her that I was not into muff diving just yet. I adjusted. I had to be tougher here because this was not my turf. I had to show these bitches that I could hold my own. It was okay. It was good. I handled it. I fit. It was the way of the street. It was the way I loved.

This was a seriously rank joint I must say. It was co-ed but we never seen the men, just on the bus. I don't even think it is there anymore. I was awaiting court in this rickety building. Remember those dangerous women I told you about well this is where I met them. We fit, as usual. These broads were just plain nasty and I loved them. They were some heavy broads and I don't mean in weight. I played hardball and did as I wanted again. I had to maintain my rep. I had to build it in the short time I had. I had to be remembered. I was so proud of myself. Life was sweet. I spent countless birthdays and holidays inside, but it was cool. I did not care not in the least. I had what I had, no more nor any less. I was important. I was finally somebody. At last I was what I wanted to be. I am not quite sure what that was but whatever it was

Life In Jail: A World All It's Own

there. For me this was big time. I was in jail and surrounded by some of the most dangerous women that I would ever meet. I tried so hard to find my place in this world and just kept fucking up everywhere I went. There was no place not even in jail that would be safe, I just did what I thought was best no more no less. There was never any end to the destruction of my life. I went hard and I went long. I held such a fear in my heart that I cannot explain, but it was there. I so wanted to be loved. I so wanted to be accepted, so I did whatever I was asked. I very rarely said no. I lived in a constant fear, I thrived on it and I prospered from it, but only by negative means. Sometimes I would just sit in my cell all alone. I just wanted to be alone. I would wish for death but it never came. Somehow I was spared and to this day I still have no idea why. These women I loved taught me a few things about crime. It was perfect. I was always willing to learn. I was also on the Methadone program because I was a junky and I needed my stuff. Well ya know really I could have gone without it. I mean I was a junky all right but if I wanted to I could have handled a bit of pain. I mean I was only doing the junk when I could get it. There would be days with plenty or with nothing. And then there were the Valium or Fioirnal or Tuinals days so yeah I was addicted to a variety of things. Heroin was cheap yet expensive back then. $30.00 a pop. It was great. I did score Meth in Oakalla because there you had to be addicted to Heroin and so I was but naturally I bullshitted who wouldn't. Legally I was high every day and at night I was given something to put me to sleep. Yes I was in heaven or was it hell, who knew or who cared, not I. I loved being in jail because I was somebody. I was looked up because I was Saskatchewan stuff. I had made my mark. I did not let anyone mess with me and I called a spade a spade.

What I hated most about jail was the slamming of the cell doors, the bells and shit. To this day I hate bells. It drove me nuts. It was like being in a black hole a deep dark black hole an endless pit of self-mutilation and horror. I use to be so scared but I never let anyone know. I was too solid. I could never show my weakness, it was not acceptable. To be weak was extremely not cool. At night sometimes I would just curl up on my bunk and cry. I never saw any really bad shit in jail unless I caused it. Back in the day it was cool. When I first went to jail there were only about seventeen broads in there, so it was nice. This was back in Prince Albert. There were no ax murderers or serial killers just a lot of fucked up broads with no life. The odd time a broad would get fucked up because she was a goof or a snitch. Once in a while broads would escape because they were bored. It was jail nothing spectacular ever happened. The worst thing I ever done was to muscle the little white girls for their canteen. I didn't know any better or did I? As I mentioned I was comfortable in jail. Sad but true. Bells,

An Arrow In My Heart

rules, lights, uniforms, and regulations conditioned me. I held myself together so good inside, but as soon as I was out it would be pure hell in no time. I mean of course the day I would get out I would get high, drunk and laid. Same old same old. If anything I was consistent.

I accepted everything that I got. I met a lot of women in jail like me so it was the cat's ass. I do not think I ever met anyone that I can call enemies. One girl in particular was my bud and she was a little white girl but she was one crazy bitch and we hit it off. She was quite the girl I must say. Right bugged out. Right up there with Chucky Manson and the boys, I paved my way. She was the one who dressed up as my pimp at the Halloween gala. Anyway we were all in the dining room having our evening meal. Our table was about three away from where the screws were seated. We were just sitting, laughing, and shooting the shit during our meal. You know trying to make the best of a bad situation. Desert was lemon meringue pie. So I'm looking at my girl and I thought to myself, I wonder if she would let me hit her in the face with this pie? So I ask her, "Hey honey I have never hit anyone in the face with pie can I do it to you?" She is as fucked up as I am if not more so and agrees. I grabbed the back of her head and boom pie in the face. It was great and it felt good too. The dining room breaks up and our table is nuts. My girl knocks over her chair jumping up to run to the washroom before the screws (guards) see what is up. Everyone is on their feet and running over to our table because they figured there was a fight. Meantime it's only the old pie in the face trick. Fuck it was funny. This girl would have done anything just like me. We were a match made in prison. She was just the kind of street people that I thrived on. Whenever I went to Saskatoon I would visit her and we'd get high. I remember once we were at her joint fixing Ritalin and Talwin. She used to fix in her jugular. I never did Talwin though just straight Ritalin. So anyway I had to lie on the stairs upside down so she could get my jugular good. I could feel the blood rushing to my head and I was exhilarated. She was doing her stuff and you know I don't even remember the rush but it must have been good. A little while later I snapped out of it and I'm in my other girl's kitchen helping her with the dishes. She told me that I was fucked up and they figured I was going to croak so she had to walk me. I guess they all did. She said I was talking and all but I don't remember a thing, but was I fucking stoned. I guess after I was fixed up I landed up flat on my back and

stayed there for a while, but I did come to. I wish I could have remembered that rush, I really do. Fixin' in my jug was not my favorite place and I never did it again.

Another time I went to jail for six months for stealing from one of Regina's supposedly finest lawyers. I would tell you his name but just in case he happens to be in a bookstore and sees this he may sue my ass so I'll keep his name a secret. All I can say is that he is extremely good in some areas. I am not sure what time it was but it was dark so it must have been at night. I wanted to go to a party but I did not have a ride. God knows why I never just took a cab. I was too messed up to give a shit. All I knew was that I was going to this party one-way or the other. I figured I'd wait around for a while and someone I knew had to come along sooner or later. Besides that I figured I might as well turn a couple of more tricks so that I had some cash. The party would still be there, so I decided to take my time. Our party's lasted long.

I was outside the Hotel walking up and down the stroll attempting to look delicious or something, you know the rules. I see this beat up older station wagon parked across the street and I thought I seen a body, well not really a person but a trick and I figured there was money so I sauntered sexily over to the car. I bent over looking the best I could with what I had but there was no one there, just the keys! Talk about luck or what. I looked up and down the street and I could see no one. I went back over to the side of the building to stand and wait until maybe someone would come to claim their mobile. I waited about fifteen to twenty minutes and no one came – to get my car! So I jumped in without even thinking hey I can't drive, but I did anyway. You see I never used my head for anything rational other than scamming. I had no license. I had no idea how to drive a mobile. I wasn't even sure how to start the damn thing. As I sat behind the wheel I was thinking in my head how the hell I could get to where I was going the shortest way. I wanted the fastest easiest route; because God knows I did not want to miss anything. I thought hey I might as well do a few more fire just to spice up the ride I was about to take. Away I went in this lawyer's beat-up ass old car. By the way what was his car doing down by one of Regina's sleazy hotels, h-m-m! The plot thickens, but I guess we will never know. Perhaps he was a trick. Some lawyer's were just ask me. Oh! Well, I get the car going and figure out how to shift and shit and there I am off to see the wizard. I was heading onto South Railway, which is now Saskatchewan Drive, towards the old train station, which is now Casino Regina, going about sixty or seventy miles an hour and some cops showed up. Damn! Busted! I thought to myself now what do they want from me? Could it be that I was going a million miles an hour down a business street or what? Or better yet, could it be that I had no license and that I could have hurt someone? Or could it be that

I had just stolen a car, what, what could they possibly want this time? I got up to the Post Office before I came to a screeching halt. I did not want to crash so I gave in – again.

I hit my head on the inside of the windshield and bounced back but I never felt it. I turned off the car and just sat there waiting for them to come, besides I was so stoned I could not really move fast, my fire was kicking in. There were two of them and they called me by name I felt so special. I was on a first name basis at all points. Yeah I was pretty important. The one guy says, "Okay Sharon whose car you got?" Naturally I said it was mine and we all laughed. He told me to get out and stand by "my" car and he was smiling. They did not bother to ask me to walk a straight line because in getting out of the car I fell out so they knew I was fucked up. The fall gave them a little hint of what shape I was in. Again, we merely all laughed and one of them helped me up off the ground. After all I did have a dress on. Plus I could not get up. The second cop is checking out the car and he begins to laugh his ass off like a mad hyena. I'm too stoned to give a shit or to figure out anything and besides I was worried about those twenty other pills I had on my person. I was thinking if they find my candy they'd either charge me or throw it away so I just ate that candy all up. I was not handcuffed yet so I slowly reached in my pocket and had a snack. I was a pro I could swallow any type of pill bare back any day. You can imagine how zonked I was a little while later. The cop comes out of the car and says to me, "Sharon do you know whose car you have?" I said, "Yeah mine and I don't give a fuck." Well he says, "You better give a fuck because you're going to jail." He proceeded to tell me about the lawyer and I thought fucking bingo, and here I go again off to the trenches. Of all cars to steal it had to be his. When I did something I didn't fuck around. I did it up right. You see there was just no end to the madness.

Someone had dared me to call him and ask him to be my lawyer. I mean I could not turn down a dare now could I. I called him, explained what had happened and asked him if he would represent me. He said sure and then asked me my name. I told him who I was and he told me to fuck off and he hung up. The guy obviously had no sense of ha ha now did he? To make a long story short, I went to court and in the courtroom this prominent lawyer brushed by me and says, "Your going away for two years bitch." Such language. I told him to eat me and I smiled. But I was a little worried because I thought I might get a long stretch out of this one. Fortunately, for me, the Judge was in a good mood that day. The Judge was looking at my file and shaking his head and I felt a bit of panic. He then looked up and said, "Well Miss Acoose you have an extensive record for one so young, blah, blah, blah, yada, yada, yada, and I have no choice but to sentence you to 6 months in The Grove for Women". I could have given the man a blowjob. I guess because I was a good girl and never missed a court appearance and all he decided to give me a break. The lawyer whose car I stole was just fucking livid. He was beside himself with anger as I walked out with such a short bit of time to do. I am sure I seen fire come out his ass. And, yet again I got away with something; I mean six-months was a duck walk, just a teaser. I figured I was pretty lucky and I took my six-months most graciously. As the cop escorted my ass by the lawyer I blew him a kiss and winked. Good story. I got a million.

Christmas in jail had to be the worst of all. It was more boring than anything else. It was lonely, maddening, sickening, deadening, hopeless, remorseful, and desperate. You spent all you time doing just that, time. No calls. No visits. No nothing. There would be times when the drugs would not even get in so it made it more boring. We were just a bunch of messed up girls all feeling the same way about a day that is supposed to be about the best day of the year. Being locked up at Christmas time really is a bitch. There was only the stupid music and, of course, the traditional meal. You would eat until you went to your cell and puked and then go back for more. At least the food was good inside and there was lots of it; a good thing because, you know, there were times I would not have too much on the outside at Christmas.

I remember one time we got some dope in and we were all fixing. It comes to my turn and of course I do too much and I fucking overdosed. Shit all I remember after they brought me out of it were broads running all over the place panicking and shit because I went under. I was being dragged around because I couldn't walk. It was crazy shit and they did look after me. It was a good thing I didn't have an enemy in there! I remember another time too that I went into some mean delirium tremors (DT's). I got scooped on a weekend as usual. Flown up north to da Grove on a Monday and by the following Thursday boom, I'm gone into space. It was the craziest shit ever. I remember coming too and I was crawling along the wall in South G. I was looking under a door that was actually a closet but I see my pops driving his trusty red tractor pulling a garbage bin, and out at The Grove no less. What my pops wouldn't do?

There was this matron that was really hormonal. She had fur on her face, and lots of it. I don't know why she just never shaved that shit off but she did not, and during my DT's I was talking to her but thought it was a man. I was talking to everything and anything. One of my favorite matrons was not on duty and I was demanding to see her, but they wouldn't do shit. I just wanted to see her. I knew she would understand. Understand what? Well I am not too sure. They didn't lock me up at night either; they let me roam around because they didn't want

An Arrow In My Heart

me going nuts. They didn't put me in segregation for the same reason. It was around midnight, I think, and I started yelling for my favorite matron. After I had come out of it, the next morning, we talked. She said in all her days of looking after women in jail she had never ran into this before. I had yelled out her name like I knew she was there and that was freaky to her. I am not sure what my sista's thought but no one treated me any different, in fact they would walk by my cell to make sure I wasn't hanging (that would come later).

And one day or night during this fiasco I was in my cell hiding and I think I was trying to sleep but I kept hearing voices. I was sweating bullets and just soaked. I would toss and turn to cover my head but the voices were loud and I heard a thumping sound. So I jumped up on my bed and looked out the window. There was a field out back with a big red industrial sized garbage bin. Here's where things went sideways. I could see people walking back and forth with shit in their hands, but I couldn't make out what they were carrying. I jumped off my bed went out into the hallway and went back in to look out the window. My eyes finally adjusted and what I seen, as the Creator is my witness, was people carrying pieces of human flesh. I could see bone and skin. I could see their heads, their brains, and lots of blood. I could see legs, arms, and sagging flesh. I fucking freaked right out at that point I was gone. I was screaming bloody murder. But it was only in my mind that I was screaming and shit. What I really done was jump under my blankets and covered my head. At one point, within this nightmare, one of those people walking back and forth stopped and turned their head and pointed at me. I thought I was next.

What a trip. This started on a Wednesday-Thursday and by Monday morning I started coming out of it and I even had one of the matrons tell me that I should write a book. I remember talking to one of the girls and told her that Dr. Gloom was going to come see me, now who the fuck was Dr. Gloom? I cannot believe that I survived this mess but I did and I would carry on. I was the talk of The Grove for a while. I am sure others had DT's but never like mine apparently. Why have I remembered this is even crazier! I could not eat. I could not sleep. They just let me walk through the doors of hell and I stayed there for five long days. It was very bizarre and is a story to be told.

I remember one time I was picked up on a weekend, as usual, and they kept us in RCMP Bucket in the old Post office in Prince George. I had me some visitors and they brought me a bunch of Tuinals. I proceeded to take them all and ended up in the hospital. I should have saved them but oh no miss greedy. I was always on the take. Always had a plan of action and a theory to commit whatever I had to commit. I never thought too clearly. For example this one time, one of my BFF's and I broke into the therapists office and we put his desk in the middle of the floor and packed all his furniture on that desk. I mean we had to find something to amuse ourselves with while we were locked up, right? I also use to steal stuff from the craft room. I really didn't have to steal but like I said I always had a research plan of some kind. And I needed something to do besides it helped the boredom.

These women I would meet we were all cut from the same cloth, it was eerie. I met women I wanted to be like, who were my heroes. I wanted to be a feared and tough bitch. I wanted to be noticed. I wanted people to cross the street when they saw me coming. Eventually I would believe I was all of these things, and with each time I ended up in jail my skin got tougher and I got wiser as far as street life was concerned. I would go to jail with my family members, and I would make some really awesome friends among the other Indian women, and even among the white girls. I met this one white girl, she was alright, and she would have to make her mark too. We were two peas in a pod. Every once in a while we would pick on the white girls, but it was all fun and games. Going to jail was like a rite of passage where you graduate from one sick place to the next. Thank god I never ended up in a Federal Institution. As sure as there is ink on these pages I would have never made it out; I would have died.

It was lonely. The darkness would creep in your cell at night and take hold. I would lay there in my cell thinking, "What the fuck am I doing here in jail?" I felt hopeless and lost. But as soon as that cell door opened at 7:00 A.M. that tough bitch Sharon had to wake up. I had to look good no matter what. I did my time. My first time in The Grove I think there were seventeen or eighteen of us, and sixteen or seventeen of those would be Indian or Métis women. We all had a story. I think in all the time I spent behind those walls I had one visitor. I went to socials, I worked, and I was a model inmate. I even got my GED-10 behind those bars. I will never forget the loneliness that kicks in; it's like losing someone. You have lots of time to think—and that was the problem. On the street you didn't have time to think, you were always busy doing this or that. But in jail it's static with nowhere to go and nothing to do. It is all dead time. I spent time in jail because I had no idea of any other way to live. I would fuck up and try to hide, but the police always get their man or woman. You can run, but you can't hide.

I remember I used to write poetry in my cell, and this one guard, she kept all my stuff. They were pretty decent, the guards—matrons is what we used to call them—and then every once in a while a bitch would come in and think her uniform actually meant something and the fight was on. I hated those guards, they caused nothing but shit. I ended up in the hole for ten days because this bitch guard was fucking with me, and she knew I couldn't do nothing. Not really sure what happened, but I know I called her out. I think it was the one or two o'clock count, and we had to go to our cell doors to be counted. She was telling me, "Okay Acoose, move it, it's time for count." I was standing in the hallway talking to one of my sista's, and I said, "Yeah, yeah, I'm going." And I've got to tell you, I just hated it when they called me Acoose. I think it was the way they said it with such authority, and I defied authority, no one told me what to do. To further the mayhem, apparently I didn't move fast enough, and she gave me a nudge. Well, the fucking fight was on, and I went in guns a blazing. I remember feeling the anger right from the tip of my toes to the top of my head; it was surreal. We are yelling, and I am acting like a banshee fresh out of hell. The director came and calmed shit down, but I ended up with a ten-day stint in the hole. Fuck I was mad. You know, guards can really be assholes, let that be known as the truth.

But at least I didn't go to SEG (segregation), the hole, you know… me time. I am not sure what happened but it was another guard trying to be someone and prove she was tough. I would get ten-days in my cell, and I was livid. I could feel the fury rise right up into my throat. Once my cell door closed I flipped out and trashed everything and ended up just sitting there on the floor crying. I mean really, who was I hurting? Certainly not them, but I sure did a number on myself. I remember thinking, "Fuck it, I am done." I ripped up my sheet, made a noose, and tied it around my neck and around the bar in the closet. I proceeded to hang my ass, and I sat ever so slowly to the ground. I could feel the sheet getting tighter, and I was seeing stars and could not breathe. Then suddenly there was a loud crash and there I was on the floor. I realized what happened and I started crying then laughing all at the same time—the bar couldn't sustain my weight, it had broken in half. I could not even kill myself properly, but the way I look at it now is that the Creator did not want me; He had a plan for me that I did not know about at the time.

So it was my rite of passage to go to jail. It was there that I would build my name, earn respect and be somebody—or so I thought. Sometimes I would be thrown in segregation. I felt like an animal. Not all the guards were horrible, but as I progressed and got older many of the good guards would move on. I, on the other hand, kept going back. I remember when it was time to be released, I was up in the front waiting for my ride, and the guards would say, "Well Acoose, see ya next time." I would laugh it off, but they were right, I would be back in. There were very few programs in there too. I mean, you could work in the kitchen, in the yard, in the laundry, and go to school or AA, but that was it. I never heard about reintegration or about how I could possibly stay out of jail. The shrink or social worker or therapist, whatever he was, would talk to us, but it was just talk. No one told me about trying to stay sober or staying out of jail. There is more to this story, but we will save it for another time and place.

CHAPTER 6

More Tales Of Woe From The Dark Side

More Tales Of Woe From The Dark Side

So with my family is all dead and gone, and my life was in turmoil. From the men, to the drugs and the alcohol, to prison, to whatever came next. I was there; I was always there. I rarely missed a thing. I never knew. Shit just happened and I would merely roll over and go on. Life was nothing short of being psychotic. And, so my father would be the last to leave me. Poor Sharon. It was always me. I pretty much handled this last death the same as all the others, insanely. I got loaded to the max. I lived relentlessly. I lived in fear of me. I lived in denial. I blamed everyone and everything around me and never took responsibility for any of my actions. I couldn't have cared less if I lived or perished. What did it matter? Even though I had children I still never gave a shit. They were anchors, but I never let them hold me back from the destruction I would encounter. Nothing or no one would be a ball 'n' chain. I mean I should have never had children but I did. I am very grateful for them and I have suffered all my life for what I have done to them. But what do you do? Not much you just move on. I did love them so, but they became products of the system, because I could not look after them. It was too late for me to even consider being a parent. Who was I trying to kid? I did what I wanted but I could not do anything about the government stepping in and stealing my babies. I gave up. Life was so unbelievable. How I survived well I'll never know. I was at my own mercy. I was at the crossroads of my life and did not know which way I should go. I made my own laws, my own rules. I had an agenda all of my own. I was on a mission. What I said was what went for me. What I did was what I did, nothing more nothing less.

   I remember when I use to work in the bar but not just as a hooker. I had actually gotten jobs as a waitress and a bartender; it was a trip, the cat's ass really. I have I told you where I got that saying from, "the cat's ass". Or didn't I? Either way, I got it from my friend who I was hired with me at the Correctional Centre. He was a gem. We became very close and I love him. He would always say this and I thought it was so cute so I'm using it. Anyway back to the story. I did my first stint as a server in a bar called the Alexandra Hotel. It doesn't even stand there anymore. It went down years ago. I was not even legal age but back in the day no one gave a shit about nothing. I was pretty good at slinging beer and selling dope at the same time. I liked what I did; it gave me recognition and importance. And, we all know that I was somebody. I had all kinds of access to alcohol and drugs, so what more could I ask for; especially being an addict. I was in all my glory. I did not get drunk all the time but I was high all the time and I would have the odd shot of Comfort. I would turn tricks on coffee and lunch breaks, and then I'd go back to serving on the floor. It was a win/win type situation. I mean I worked in a bar what else was there to do? Can you imagine that drinking and doping all the days of my life? It

An Arrow In My Heart

was bizarre but it was an honest living, sort of. One time a bunch of steelworker's came in after their hard day cutting steel or whatever it was they did. There were a couple tables of them and they sat in my section, lucky me and lucky them. It was fabulous. They were serious tippers and one of them would become my regular "sugar daddy". What a treat.

These men were ordering booze like we were going to run out, thirsty-little-devils they were! Finally they began to filter out one by one and by around 7:00 in the evening they were all gone until the next payday. I was cleaning up their tables. You know putting glasses away, getting tables back in their proper places, dumping ashtrays and such. Low n' behold I found a wallet under one of the tables. One of the guys must have dropped it. It was my lucky day and his loss. I never told anyone and I took a break. I went into the washroom and in this wallet was about $700.00 or more dollars give a buck or two; giddy-up, I scored! I then took the wallet and destroyed all the shit inside and dumped it in the canister out back of the place. I never thought for a moment this man might need the money for stuff. No I just did what I wanted. I did not think perhaps he had a family to feed. Finder's keeper's loser's weepers. Really I should have done the right thing but I did not know what that was. I figured that I had done the right thing. I found it and I keep it. Simple. He did come back to the bar looking for his lost wallet but nope no one seen it, no one atoll. Fancy that this was the one who would become my regular trick. What a lucky guy. He even asked me once to marry him and all I could say was, "Fucking gross". He really was a very nice looking man but he was a trick not really a man right? You would never marry a trick unless you were desperate or stupid or both. But I did let him be my sugar daddy. He kept the money flowing and that was all that mattered. I kept him on a string by telling him that maybe one day I would marry him. I had to keep him around somehow right? And this stuff too is my opinion and mine alone. You know there have been women who got with their tricks deeper and its how they rolled. I mean that ain't shit ya can do about who you dig trick or no. It ain't no thang. But me, nah it wasn't my thang. Who wanted a man with a job and money, fuck not me!

Everyone and everything was at my mercy. I remember once I was even creamed by a car right on Victoria Avenue and McIntyre Street. Me, my flavor of the week and his bud or our bud were on our way to get more happy booze like we needed it. I do not remember being smoked by the car but it happened. How in the fuck I did not die, well that I will never know. I woke up the next day and the guy I was with was there at my side, how noble. It was cool I guess. He cared enough to at least show some support. I was in pain, lots of pain. My right leg had been busted up pretty bad and it was swollen beyond repair at the moment and it had to wait to be casted. I was in traction for a good week. It was so sore that I did not even complain right away.

The guy, my flavor of the week, kinda like a catch of the day, had come to tell me that he was leaving for British Columbia without me. He did not want to wait because he just wanted to leave. I told him that I would meet him there. I told him I loved him. He told me he loved me and he was gone like a thief in the night. By-the-by he too belonged to another. It's just a never-ending story. He was in shock that I actually made it through this alive. That is why he came to the hospital, he was amazed. He told me he tried to pull me back but it was too late. Apparently I flew over the top of the car and I ended up flat on my back with my leg bent all out of shape, grotesquely positioned under me. I never felt a thing. He figured I was dead but I was only knocked out from the impact of hitting the pavement. I woke up sick, confused and in dying pain. But alas the nurse was there every couple hours with a trusty hefty shot of good ole morphine. Yes that's right I had died and gone to heaven, again. Once again legally I was high for about seven weeks. It was great.

I was in the hospital for about eight to twelve weeks because I could not catch on to walking in those stupid crutches. It took about two weeks before they even put a cast on. The cast was from the top of my leg to my toes. It was wicked because they had to teach me to walk all over again, so naturally I would play the duck in order to get more dope. What they would do was give me a shot to ease the pain and then take me to therapy. And again, here I would become somebody. The nurses back in those days really gave a shit and they liked me because I always had a good sense of humor. It worked for me. As a matter of fact my humor has been instrumental in my sobriety.

My doctor had been away for quite some time and when he came back the shit hit the fan because I was still on the morphine. What can I say the nurses liked me? He just went wild and the poor nurses all felt his wrath. Of course I was immediately cut off morphine and given Tylenol #3. All good things did have to come to an end. I was happy. Once the good shit was cut off I tired of being in the hospital and miraculously I learned to walk with my crutches. It was a miracle. The doctor gave me orders and one of them was not to drink; he was kidding right? He gave me a nice healthy prescription of drugs and away I went off to the Land of Oz. I had what I needed, drugs. He had given me some morphine and some Tylenol #3. Could I have been happier? Meantime I had almost been killed but it never sank in. Then I end up with a cast up to my ass plus I had free dope, perfect.

Anyway someone told me I should go see a lawyer and sue the guy who hit me. I cannot remember what took place but the next thing you know I get a settlement for a little better than ten grand; cha fucking ching!!! I found out later if I did not settle out of court I likely could have tripled that amount. For sure I would have been a goner. The ten grand almost killed me never mind more. I had to give my lawyer some of the scratch but not much. Things were relatively cheap back in the day. Ten grand was a lot of money especially for a nineteen year-old junkie.

All I knew was that I was fucking rich. Nineteen years old and I had near 10K in my little tacky mitts. Can you imagine that? I also had lots of pals although I really did not part with too much of my scratch. I remember once being in the Kitchener Hotel and someone wanted a light. As smooth as I am, I roll up a hundred-dollar bill torched up the end and lit their smoke. No brains no pain. Next thing you know, I'm on a plane on my way to Vancouver with a pit stop in Calgary. I hooked up with one of my cousins in Regina, who by the way does not remember any of this, but we went. We stayed at her sister's, kept it mildly calm but did kick it into the party mode here and there. We stayed there for about a week. I only had one hangover and it lasted for about a week so that was cool. Nice, very nice. I remember we went to a movie. Guess which one? The Exorcist. I'll tell you that did me in. I almost puked right in the theater but I waited until I got outside and then I let it rip. Would you believe that tough old Sharon Acoose had to sleep with the lights on? I was severely messed up but it was a gross fucking show back in those days. It was always interesting to say the least.

I did a few things while in Calgary. I took out my cousin's kids a lot and spent lots of money on them and we had a ball. It was fun. Then we took off of Vancouver. I had to go see my man. You know the one. He was with me when I got wiped out by the car. Who knows maybe he pushed me. Anyway I tracked him down and let him know where I was. You know if I wanted to get laid I could have stayed in Regina but oh no I always had to go to extremes. I rented a room for a week and had some fun. I only had him with me once but that was good enough. I had bigger fish to fry. I am not sure if it was the men who made me feel good or if it was my expertise as a hooker, whatever, I made it good. I mean yeah I never had a serious amount of orgasms but the foreplay was always a blast. The guy I was with got mad at me and left. Apparently he was in for the money but I almost died for it so why should I give it to anyone. I got sex and that is all I wanted at the time. The thing is I was not about to pay for any nooky. No not me. I would move on, as did he.

So I just went on a big party alone and had a great time. I spent some time with my cousin boasting and shit because it was part of our life. Even though we had money we still went stealing. Made sense to me. I had never been to the West Coast so I did appreciate the weather. It was simply marvelous. I never went sightseeing except the inside of the bars and it was rude. I met a lot of cool people and even some I knew from Regina. Birds of a feather. The only way to fly. I first tried heroin here but would not do it again until later in my career, like I said earlier I would do heroin with my Uncle. I was only nineteen or so. I might have been older. I really did not know too much really about anything. I mean I thought I did. But there was a whole big world in front of me I had no idea about, but I would drastically find out, that was for sure. Vancouver was a trip and I met the right folk or should I say wrong folk, as usual. I was like a magnet to these people and I thrived on them, as they did on me. They were my reason for living and breathing at the time. It was essential for me to be with these people because I had to learn how to live their way. I was like a sponge. I soaked up all that I could so that I could be the best at what I was.

My existence depended on them. Finally, I was running out of cash so I decided to go home rather than get stuck in Vancouver. I had little less than a grand left and I thought I best get my ass back to Saskatchewan. I mean I could have turned tricks and I did but not as much as usual. I had decided that since I had all this money that I'd take a little break from the street. I also decided to take a train home so that I could see some of the countryside. I figured I might as well get something out of this ten grand. If only I would have known better I may have been very rich by now but it was not meant to be. The trip was okay. I do not remember too much of it because I spent a lot of time in the drinking car and partied with the bellboys and porters or mascots or whatever it is they are called. I was driven by some unknown force to always surround myself. Men they were all tricks as far as I could see it, and I would get what I wanted from these men on this train. The situation was never any different. I ended up tricking some of these guys so really the trip was not all lost even though I did not see too much. You cannot really see too much lying on your back now can you? No matter where I went I was always on the take. Money was a big thing for me and I would do anything to get it. My life was something. The only good thing I done with my cash was that I bought my deceased brother Joey a headstone for his grave. All the rest was spread across western Canada.

I also worked as a bartender/waitress at the Wascana Hotel. It was just as whacked out as the other bar job I had. I was always severely messed up. However, needless to say, regardless of how fucked up I was I still made some nice coin as a waitress believe it or not. I just acted cute and cuddly plus I learned to short change like a bitch. I was just a gem. I never ripped off my own, just the business folk that came in. They were easy. I also had a trick room upstairs and when a regular came in I'd just take a break, do my stuff, and be back on the floor in about ten to fifteen minutes. Quick I was. It was cool. I had all kinds of cash all the time but I was still broke. All my earnings from the street and my jobs went back into my body somehow, either by lethal injection or by liquid. Didn't matter to me as long as I got what I wanted.

This is also the bar that my girl and I would mess up. It was after the death of my brother and I was attempting to be a fucking hero. It was a vendetta or something. We were in the bar just pissed to the gills and getting rowdier by the minute. My boss did try to get me to settle down. He told me I could have a room to sleep it off in but I informed him that fuck all was wrong. But oh no he said the wrong thing and boom we both snapped at the same time. At least we had some momentum happening. After all we were street sisters and did most things together. The next thing you know shit is airborne. The beer glasses were stacked three high on the bar and those went flying. We just lost our minds. My pal was chucking chairs, ashtrays, and anything else she could throw and I'm right there doing the same. It was total chaos. We demolished the bar in minutes. Meantime while all this is going on my boss and his wife are hiding in the beer cooler under cover so as not to get whacked with any flying objects. He never fired me for this little episode because I was a great booze pusher. I did have to sit it out for two weeks, but then he let me back in. I had to work for about a month or so for free to pay for the damages to the bar, but it was a small price to pay for what I did. I did not care because I still had my trick room so I made up for what I lost. I always had a backup plan no matter what. I could have very well gone to jail but my boss liked me, didn't everyone?

I was the bartender and waitress at the Champs Hotel. I remember with all these jobs I always had my own supply of booze and dope tucked away in the cooler in a safe place. I drank Southern Comfort because Janice Joplin was god. Joplin was the cat's ass! I admired and sought to be like her, excluding the singing. I was always half-baked. I did well at what I was doing always. I was an expert in my life but only on the street. If I would have kept doing a good job my boss would have made me bar manager, but of course I fucked this up like everything else in my world. I remember one night I got so drunk at work it was not even funny. I had blacked out and I do not even remember closing the bar, that's how fucked up I was. And somehow I misplaced over a grand of my till float. I thought fuck I've had it now but I'd worry about it later, you see I had a party to attend and I could not be late by any means, right, right?

I still made it to work the next day. How I'll never know. I was sick as a dog so I went to my stash and fixed myself up. I had to do this something so I could open up my bar on time. Plus I had to clean up a little and try finding my lost cash. I was lucky no one had gotten there before me, especially my boss. I had time to get it together and make it look like fuck all happened. Once I had seen what I had done I begin to panic. I had a few more shots of Southern and some more pills to take off the edge. I mean I was short fucking near a grand. It was reason to drink right? My boss would be in any time to pick up my night deposit and I did not have it. So I scurried about knocking shit over in a frenzy trying to find my loot. I looked all over the place, in the garbage, in the coolers, like it would really be there, but you never knew with me it could have been anywhere. I looked high and I looked low. Then I thought oh God what if I took and partied with it, man when I fucked up I did it up right for sure. Finally after running my ass off I opened up the till and what do I find, yes that's right I found my float. I had stuck it far under the tray, so I am assuming that I put it there for safekeeping. I mean how I would know since I was pissed to the gills, well I have no idea. So there it was my sorry ass was saved yet again. Plus there was well over a grand so I made up my float and kept the loose change. So really we were all ahead and no one had to know any better. The day moved on. I don't know but somehow I came out on top. I didn't have just the horseshoe up my ass, I had the whole horse up there. Anyway, I was eventually fired from this bar, plus barred, because I was a bad actor. Only God knows what I did. Apparently I came to work all fucked up, big surprise, and someone did something to a family member and I fixed them up. I beat them with my tray. I was nice enough until I fell off the edge and this was a regular occurrence. God I thought I was so perfect. I was so someone. I was the girl, straight up. I was tough. I didn't give a shit about this job or any other job for that matter. There were lots of other jobs plus I was still hooking so it's not like I would be broke. Plus I had embezzled money and of lots it from this bar. Always on the take I was. So, as I said, I would be fired; oh well. I never ended up in jail because I busted up some bitch. Someone was looking after me that was for sure. I realize today that it was God, my love, my Creator, my life. I will be forever grateful. Pity was truly taken upon me by the Creator. By the way none of these old bars even stand anymore, but I do! I am so thankful that I never died along with them. There were plans made for me I just did not know what they were until now.

    Speaking of old bars that are no more, I also worked in a fine establishment called the Queen's Hotel. Same old, same old. I was always messed up in some way shape or form. To an alcoholic/ drug addict, working in these places was the cat's ass. It was perfect. It went hand in hand. Kinda like salt and pepper or the needle and the juice. I mean in my mind I wasn't doing anything wrong. I had a job or jobs. Little

An Arrow In My Heart

did I know, at the time, that I was simply feeding my own addictions! In these bars, in this life, I was somebody. People looked up to me because I had made a name for myself. Yeah I had enemies but my good friends outnumbered my bad ones. This world was my domain. It was where I ruled. If I didn't like someone who came into "my" bar I just would not serve them. I'd just move onto the next. There were other waitresses around so who gave a shit, not me. After all I was the chosen one. I was important one. Life went along and I went with it whether it be good or bad. Whatever happened happened, and that was that. I remember after my brother was murdered, people called me a rat because I testified in court. Whatever. I really did not give a fuck. People would forget and so would I. They could call me anything they wanted except late for supper. I didn't ask for my brother to be shot now did I? So fuck all y'all!!

As I look back I have no idea why I was spared. Many times I have fondled death's door only to rip him off. Just when he figured I would be his, the hand of God would pull me back. I know today it was not luck it was my fate, my destiny to survive. God had a plan for me and it was certainly not to perish. I believe in fate and that is what it was, my fate. Plans for my life were previously made it would just take thirty some years to put it all in to perspective. I had to live through all the shit and abuse in order to prosper and help others. I had to live in pain. I had to live in fear. I had to live in absolute despair to be who I am today. I know this and I have accepted this. I have no regrets for the way I lived because of how much I have accomplished. It has not been easy but it has been necessary. I am who I am through the hand of God.

I lived in constant fear of who I was and of other's. There was nothing I could have done to prevent the events that took place in my life, in my world, in the way I lived. I was very generous to myself at everyone else's expense. I always had what I wanted but never what I needed. I did for me and only me. I remember my childhood. I remember my adolescents. I remember my life. I remember all the sorrow and all my losses. It saddens me and yet I have prospered in a new beginning. I can now put it all behind me. I can use what I have brought from my past and help others who are in despair because I have been there. I always knew there was a reason for my life and how it was lived. Every day and every night I am thankful to God for taking pity on my sorry ass. So, now apparently, it is time to move on into the present with the hope the future will be a little easier to cope with. I mean nothing is easy but if you accept your life it will be a smoother ride, trust me.

This one time, at Band Camp... Just kidding—need to keep the humor alive! This one time I was attacked and beaten by six of the biggest black men in the entire world. I might have been about eighteen because my deceased brother Joey was still alive. Back in the day these black men would come up from the Minot Air Force Base in North Dakota and wreak havoc. There was a war going on, and there would be few survivors. The street women would go party with them, me being one of them, and damn they were fine. There was this one dude named Doc, and lordy lordy he was fine. He actually asked me to marry him, but of course my fool ass would say no. I spent lots of time with him when he came to Regina, and I was in such lust it was crazy. Part of me wanted to go with him, but something in my mind stopped me—after all I was only eighteen years old.

Anywho, there was this one woman who I was at war with, and we had it out in front of the Kings Hotel in Regina. I kicked her ass, and I felt so powerful because I had an audience. I was calling her names—like I had any right—but my pea-brain was not working so well back then, and I was calling her a nigger lover. It was at a time when I thought I was invincible, and I was a racist. We were rolling around out front the bar just giving each other the mitts. She would go down, I would go down, and we would attack. It was like two cats on a hot tin roof. Anyway someone stopped the fight, and I remember yelling at her, "this ain't over yet bitch, you mine!" You know because she gave me a run for my money and nearly got me, but I was better, or so I thought.

Later that evening I was at a party and I was bragging about the battle I had won earlier that evening. We were all getting high—like I could get even get any higher, but I always tried. I think it was about 6:00 in the morning and the door came flying open. I was stoned on acid (LSD), and six of the biggest black men in the entire world came in with that little Indian broad I had battled the night before. She pointed at me and said, "There she is, that fucking bitch!" My spidey-senses kicked in, and I jumped, ready to rumble. I thought, "Oh fuck, I'm dead," but I would not go down without a fight; ever. I am not sure what happened, but I could hear things crashing and screaming, blood curdling screams, and I realized they were coming from me. I remember yelling and telling her, "Bitch, if I don't die today you are fucking dead! This is never going to end and I will kill you!" I mean at least I had balls, right?

Someone finally stopped it, and I ran to the bathroom. Remember now, I was stoned on acid so my wounds looked extreme. I was trying to clean up my face—it was hideous. I happened to look at the door, and one of those gigantic black men was standing at the door pointing a gun at me, and I thought, "What the fuck?" I looked at him, and he fired the gun. I fell to the floor like a sack of potatoes, and they all ran out the door because they figured he'd killed me. I remember laying on the floor in the fetal position. When I realized I wasn't dead,

I jumped up and looked for a bullet hole, but there was only a scratch on my leg. I have no idea where that fucking bullet went, but it wasn't my day to die. I remember leaving and still being so high. I was ducking and diving into bushes. All I knew is that I had to get downtown to find my brother. I found him in the Hamilton Hotel and dropped to the floor by the table. It was crazy after that. I remember telling him what happened, and I remember him carrying me upstairs to a room where he put me to bed and left me with a gun. I am not sure what he did, and that is the end of this story. I lived to tell another.

A Drug Deal Gone Wrong

The next story is about a crew of us trying to kill a drug dealer that was supposed to be a rat (a rat was a person who informed on other criminals to the police). We devised an insane plan. Another woman and I were supposed to go to his door and knock on it like we were there to pick up dope. We were then supposed to jump in the bushes, and the others would open fire and shoot his ass right there at his front door. Ahhh, the insanity! Well, the door opened but it was his mother who answered the door. We stood there not moving and wondering, "What the fuck we gonna do now?" Well that is what I was thinking; I am not sure about my home girl. Then the supposed rat appeared and stepped in front of his mother. That old girl may well have kept us out of prison.

We ended up at a party, and I was in the washroom. My acid trip was turning bad because of the shit that just transpired. I was sitting in the washroom thinking, "What the fuck, what the fuck?" I was so high, and my head was pounding. I must have started my period because I saw blood in the toilet. I let out a blood-curdling scream. Later I saw a jar of beets somewhere (I know it's crazy, but it's the mind of someone on acid), and I screamed even louder because I thought I got shot in my pussy (vagina) and that someone had put it in a jar. Yup, I was pretty much fucked right there. It was never-ending, but for me it was normal. I was a street person, and that is just the way we lived: one moment at a time, never knowing when we would live or die. I mean who thinks that way unless of course you drop an insane amount of LSD.

My Baby Boy

One time, after my sister died, I decided I wanted to go out to party. I ended up leaving my son alone sleeping in his room. I did make sure he ate and was changed, and I waited until he was fully asleep. Then away I went, off to see the wizard.

I ended up in the drunk tank, and I was worried about my son—I know it sounds crazy, but I really was worried. I didn't tell the cops my son was alone because I knew I would be let out as soon as I sobered up, which was at about two in the morning. I went back to the motel and realized I had lost my keys. I stood by the door and couldn't hear him so I thought he must be okay, but I did hear a party happening on the next floor so away I went. I partied all night and when I woke up, there was a pile of I don't know what beside me. I slithered out of the room and snuck downstairs. I found a cleaning lady, and she gave me a key to get into my room. I will never forget what I saw!

I opened the door, and my baby boy was standing up. He must have been crying for a long time. His little face was red and swollen. He was wet from head to toe, but you know what, as soon as he saw me he started to smile and cry all at the same time. Fuck, my heart broke, and I just fell to the floor holding him tight in my arms, and we were both crying. Fuck this is damn hard—I don't know how long I sat on that floor, but we both cried. I was kissing him and holding him as close as I could. I finally got my shit together, and we had a bath. I lay back in the water after I had a fix of some drug I had. And I just watched as he played in the water. I remember thinking, "What the fuck am I doing?" I remember telling him how sorry I was, and he just loved me without any conditions at all. I believe this was one of those moments when I almost gave up the drugs—you know, surrendered to my addiction—but I didn't know where to go for help. I cried for what seemed like hours on end. This was one of those dark times when I just wished for death, and I even thought of killing him and myself. I remember telling him I would find some help, and I think I was praying. I told him I loved him, but in reality I didn't love him enough, not right then at least. We sat in the tub for a long time, and for a moment, life was normal. I cleaned him up, dressed him up, and took him out to eat. That was the last time I would see him because he was taken away from me. True stories!

I lived a long life on the street doing what street people do. I ran around with any man that would have me, and I spent about nine years in and out of jail. I lived in extreme mayhem and never knew what would happen from one day to the next. That was my life, and that is what I did. I remember waking up in my hotel room, and before my feet even hit the floor I would have a needle in my arm and a shot of Southern Comfort for breakfast. That was how my day began, and that's how it would end. That is all I did. There was nothing more, and I was not ever expected to be successful or to live a full life. I thought I would be dead by the time I was twenty years old. My life was worthless. I had no ambition, no drive. I watched as my mother died, my father died, my sister died, my brother died, and my husband died. They left me alone in this insane world to fend for myself. How the fuck was I going to do this? The only things that were important to me were drugs and alcohol, money and men. That was the order of my life. I was tough. I could take a beating, and I could give one. I stood down to no man or woman. I was afraid of absolutely nothing. If you fucked with me I would simply get you back somehow, some way. Alcohol and drugs did not leave me to go gently off into the night. Time and time again I would be stripped of my dignity and emotions. I would learn to be hard from a young tender age. I would lose both of my children. I would walk away from them and not look back. I would sign papers that deemed me an unfit mother. End of story!

I would lose my eldest daughter when she was nine months old simply because I was so fuck up that I didn't deserve to have her. I remember one time I had a visit with her and I stole her and ended up in Calgary at my uncle's house. I had to break in for that matter because he was not home. When he got home he was kinda mad but he got over it and we did heroin together, you know that family thang like having a cup of tea. I am not sure how long I stayed there but I scored welfare. I think I eventually gave and in. I had my girl sent back to her rightful owners because I could not look after shit. I was a mess and my kids would all feel my wrath. I was a horrible mother. I cared for me and only me; my kids were weights. They were thorns in my side, I didn't know any better. I didn't know any fucking better and may angels would suffer.

I tried to be a mother but that didn't work for me it was not my destiny. At the age of twenty-nine I got out of jail staying in Prince Albert and had my last daughter when I was thirty years old. And I fucking blew that too! It was not a good time and I was nowhere ready, but there she was born to a practicing addict. Times were tough. I mistreated her and I beat her. I ignored her and I left her alone. I didn't know what to do and then one day I hauled ass and headed back to Regina where things would not go any better. But it was there that our lives would change. I nearly lost her to the system, yet another child, but there was something that made me hold on to her and I did my best with what I had. She suffered trust me. She like my other children would meet my wrath. I didn't know how to love. I didn't love myself, so how could I love someone else? Even when they were my own flesh and blood?

This little girl would suffer by my hand. Fuck, oh my god, I am so sorry for what I did to my children. I didn't mean to. I hurt them beyond repair and it has taken me years and years to be able to forgive myself – but I did. I have spoken to all of them and said what had to be said. Now it's in their ballpark to accept, love and forgive. I love my children with all that I have in my heart and soul. The pages after this or the books after this will be their stories of recovery if they so choose. I cannot change the past but I sure as hell can change the future, but only mine. I have said my sorry to each of them. I paid the piper trust me I paid the piper. I love you all!

Oh and my move to Vancouver back in the early 70's can't stop without telling you that story. My BFF, Wind-in-her-hair (pseudonym) and I decided, "Hey let's move to Vancouver how bout?" I was with her brother for a time too and we would go nowhere fast as usual. He didn't do drugs but he drank like a fish and I was the drug addict. We balanced each other out. He would knock the shit outta me when I was stoned because I wouldn't feel it but I always found out and I would get him back later, always. I was water and he was fire and water put fire out! Anyway, back to Wind-in-her-hair, we talked it over and thought it would be a great notion. And back than Indian's paid only half fair on the train. So we were preparing for our trip. She had a lil girl that was two and that kid just loved me. Not sure why, but I was her hero and she would be oh shit around 40ish now. I used to call her Niecy-Pie.

We had money, so early the next morning we got up and took a train to the West Coast. We had a few bags and we also packed two 40ozs of CC for the trip. Yes we never left home without the goods. I don't remember much of the trip because I would pass out here and there. I did try to maintain myself because I had to help my BFF with the baby, but I was drunk all the way there. I even managed to make friends on the train, nudge, nudge, wink, wink. This is how my life in Vancouver would begin. Of course I would gravitate to East Hastings with all the good people, well they were good to me. Birds of a feather, right? Yes, it was my world. My way and I would try to have a life there. I know that Wind-in-her-hair hooked up with some dude that had money and I think she did ok for herself, but before that we partied a lot together. We had no place to stay so we found another friend who let us stay with her and her three kids; she had a daughter and twin boys, and it was a good time. We hung around East Hastings and I would end up going to nowhere land.

I would live on East Hastings in a pile of shit. I did heroin when it was around and I did all kinds of other shit, plus I drank. One of my friends was living there and we became close. I would be at her place all the time, she was great. I think she was one of my deceased brother's girlfriends and we were inseparable. I remember some of our friends would come from Regina to score a load or two of heroin and she would let them cut it up and package it up in her basement. This one dude would just give her the leftover heroin and she would give it to me for Christmas. Now that was my kinda present. I was in my glory. I had some of the best heroin money could buy and it was all free, cha ching. Then I got pregnant too and that is the lil dude I talked about earlier. He was born in Vancouver in July 1976. I did try so hard to be a mother but for real I had no idea how. This kid never had a fucking chance. I would fuck up his life and I am not sure if it was good or bad that he was taken from me, because only God knows the kinda life he woulda had right? I mean I was so fucked, how was I going to take care of a baby?

My friend liked to do downers and she would try to turn tricks but I would find her and rescue her. I remember this one time we were in the Sunrise on East Hastings and she was getting all stoned and I was stoned to but on the good shit. I was trying to watch but I had to pee so I left and I told this dude to keep an eye on her till I got back. I do my thing, come back and Wind-in-her-hair was gone and I hit the guy because he let her go. So out the door I went and there was this Tranny on the corner and I asked her if she seen my friend and I described her. She had seen her and she pointed in the direction she'd gone. So I went running in my Stiletto's all the while yelling her name and I could hear her. This dude had her at the train tracks and they were on the ground. I could hear her crying so I got even madder and when I got there I beat the shit out that dude, robbed him and grabbed her and hit the track. I gave her shit. She would eventually die in Vancouver while I was at my sister's funeral back in Regina around 1977. Another sister lost to the harsh realities of the street life.

I remember one time being with this dealer and we were in his room with a few other junkies. Now these people were hardcore junkies who had been into Heroin 24/7 for ten, twenty, thirty years. They didn't fuck around. I hooked up with this guy because he liked me, he thought I was cute. We were just kicking back getting high and again I nearly went under. He fixed up this shit and popped it into my vein and instantly I could feel myself floating. It was not as good as that very first time but it was good. He was talking to me because he knew what was up and just talked me out of going down for the count. It was just heaven that heroin hola snapping arseholes it was just freaking awesome! No wonder people got addicted to it for so long, dayum. Life in Vancouver was no different than anywhere else I had been. Same shit different pile. Same fuck ups all over the place. Nowhere to, go nowhere to hide, just a dismal life over and over. I remember standing in the rain on East Hastings, dope sick or hung over, trynna turn a trick to survive. It was my life and I choose to live that way. No one told me, "Sharon go be a whore, go be homeless in Vancouver or Regina." I just did it. I did it all on my own. I was my own misdemeanor. So I lived in Vancouver. I tried another man who was in another relationship. But you know me, I had to have what was not mine. Just a merry-go-round of street life.

CHAPTER 7

The Arrow In My Heart... Disappears

I interviewed a young woman a few years ago who was cut from the same cloth as me. She made this statement, so I am going to borrow it from her: "I hung up my stilettos. I made a decision. I looked at my life and at what I was doing. I was getting too old to be a prostitute anymore, and I needed something new. So the stilettos were put to rest. I was spent like an old Hollywood harlot. I had no more in me: it was time to move onward and upward." I hung up my Stiletto's.

So let's move into my change and what happened. I am not even sure where the change occurred, but it happened after I left Prince Albert. I just got tired of it there so I rented a U-Haul, filled it up, and hauled ass back to Regina—where, of course, the mayhem would continue. It took a few more years of insanity to get my shit together. My third child, a little girl, was two years old when I went home. All my people were gone already, but I still had my eldest brother and my sister-in-law who have both been instrumental in my sobriety. In all honesty I am not even sure they know how much they impacted my life, but they did, and I am forever grateful to the both of them.

I continued to drink and do drugs. I was not turning too many tricks because for the most part as men just don't want older women. I mean there are massage parlors that old broads put together, but that just was not my gig. Tricks are your husbands, your brothers, your uncles, your grandfathers, businessmen, lawyers, doctors, chiefs, and they want stuff done that their wives do not do in the bedroom. Trust me, there are some very freaky men in this world that will pay top dollar for sex in all directions. Let that be known. I lived on welfare until I regained my Indian status, and I started university in 1989.

So the lights came on and someone was actually home. It was like I struggled with a key trying to get into the door, and finally it opened just like that. My daughter was maybe five years old when I surrendered to myself and said, "Okay, it's enough, I need something different in my life." I sobered through AA (Alcoholics Anonymous) and it would change my life forever. It's not that I am promoting AA, but I am just saying it's where I would eventually find Sharon and her spirit. I did not know about culture, but that too was coming—I just had to be patient. So it took me two years to get my first real solid year of sobriety, and sobriety has been good. I started as a mature student at the University of Regina. I worked hard. I hated reading, and I could not put a sentence together for the life of me; but I never gave up. I never missed a single day of class. I never handed in assignments late. I just did what I was supposed to do. I felt so inferior though with all those white students in those huge ass classrooms. Damn they were big. One class had five hundred people in it. I kid you not. I would walk around those big ass hallways listening to the buzz of the students and I was in awe. I just couldn't believe that I was doing this.

But I did not falter, and I worked like the devil was chasing me. I was also enrolled at the Saskatchewan Indian Federated College (SIFC), now the First Nations University of Canada, and that is where I discovered what being an Indian is was all about. I fell in love with it, and I wanted more. I talked to the Elders, I joined the Student Association, and I became part of something. I never stopped talking. It was like this voice inside me just erupted, and man it was awesome. I volunteered for all the convocations, and I must tell you they were brilliant. Indians in full regalia, drummers singing the Honor and Victory song, and all those people being marched in to get their degree. I used to stand at the back of the room feeling so proud to be an Indian and I wanted that; I had to have it. OMG I wanted that so much.

I never thought it possible, but in 1993 I convocated with a Bachelor of Arts in Human Justice. It was the best thing since fry bread. My family was there with me to watch me get my degree. I was now one of those students I had yearned to be for so long. I made it. Then I thought, "Hmm, I wonder if I can do a Master's degree?" So that journey began. I applied to do a Master's of Social Work, and let me tell you this was a bit tense to say the least. But I never gave up and worked my ass off to get that degree. I would learn so much about how far I could push myself; and it was pretty far, if I do say so myself. I would run into lots of controversy. I do not want to put down the faculty; it's just that they did not know how to treat or be around Indians, that is all so it is all forgiven. I have let go.

I didn't even know how to work a computer but I learned. I would sit in my classes and look around the room and think what the hell, how did I get here? I tell ya those other students and I were from two very different world; two very different worlds. I would cringe sometimes because I didn't know what the hell they were talking about. Holy shit homeboy; bring it down a level or two. But you know what I just handled it and I did my best. I was on a mission.

I never thought it would be possible, but in 1995 I convocated with a Master's of Social Work. Yes, it was a miracle, and all because I surrendered to myself, faced my addictions. I went to AA meetings, and talked and talked and talked. It was how I survived the mayhem of my life. In the time between these two degrees, I would also be hired as a corrections officer, and I would receive a Certificate in Corrections. I would say life was going okay. I will not go into a big long story about my jobs, and such, but it is important to note that once my healing journey began, and I stayed clean, nothing was impossible for me. I pushed myself to the point where I thought I was going to lose it, but I did not. I rose from the ashes and every move I made was meant to show my children what life could be like without alcohol and drugs. I did things I never thought possible. Like I said, I thought I would be dead by twenty, and I was okay with that. I did not see. I could not imagine life other than the street, but there has always been something in my spirit that allowed me to hold on. I knew that once I began my healing journey, life would change. The lights would come on full force, and I would stand at attention. I had come out of the wilderness so to speak. Seriously, who would have thought that a prostitute from the streets could ever go this far in life? If someone would have told me forty years ago that I would be where I am now, I would have said, "Fuck you!"

The Other Side of Jail
So there it is. I obtained two university degrees and a certificate in corrections. I cannot re-e-e-ally write this book without sharing with you about my time inside. With that I mean I worked as a Correctional Worker, yes I did. I ended up on the other side of the fence so to speak, and for once I was not the one being locked up. It would not be right for me to overlook this very interesting position as a jail guard. It would be quite an adventure and a great learning experience. But on the other hand it was very strange; very strange indeed. I never thought for a moment I would ever end up in jail as a guard. I thought perhaps one day I would die in jail. I cannot begin to tell you  how much I hated those guards. It is true what they say, "What goes around comes around." I have certainly gone full circle. Weird but true!

It was during my Master's degree that I had applied for the job. I had spotted the ad in the paper. So I thought what the hell might as well give it a try. All they could say was no. So I took it upon myself to apply for the position as a Corrections Worker 1 (CW1). Sometime later I received a response in the mail and I don't think they knew what they would be up against, but they sent me a letter to let me know my application had been accepted. I was blown away. I then waited about another six weeks before I would hear from them again. This would be the letter telling me when I was up next for my interview. There were three people in the interview and me. I do not know if I was nervous because I really was not expecting to score a job; not here, not in a jail, not me. The whole process took about an hour or so. I had a good feeling about it all but so did I when I had a good poop. I answered the questions to the best of my ability and that was it. I was pretty straight forward and to the point. Then again I had some pretty good feelings about sex but nothing good ever came of that. So I did my best and I left.

So now I get a call or another letter telling me that I had a job as a CW1 at the Regina Provincial Correctional Centre. I really couldn't believe it. Of course I would be on probation and have to do training and stuff but I think I was ready. Actually I was pretty damn hyped and I have no idea why, people hate guards and I had become one; go figure. I think the exhilaration came from the fact I, Sharon L. Acoose (ex-inmate herself), was actually going to be a guard of all things. I was told there would be three phases to the training. I started my training with a group of ten or so people. They would all become my buddies and still are today. This was all very weird though. I could not shake the feeling. I mean it was not a bad weird, just weird is all. The training was off and unusual but I would make it through. I am amazed I even passed the stupid exam because it was kind of crazy to say the least. I was totally stumped by it and I already had a Master's degree, go figure.

So here I was. I became a jail guard. Is that not wild or what? Who would have thunk? Not me. If someone would have said that I would be a guard in the old days I would've said, "Get the fuck outta here. Not even." The only thing that really got under my skin was the slamming of the doors and the closing of the bars. I could not shake the old ghosts it brought out. There was a lot shit happening. Lots of old ghosts began to surface but I was okay with it. Knowing that I could walk out after a shift was all good for me. It was very spooky because the building has been standing since 1913. It had lots of character or better yet character(s). I remembered when I use to have to sit in segregation and it haunted me for a while. I could see myself behind those bars. I could see the past creeping up on me and I did not know what to do. I would feel a chill; the chill of the ghosts and the fear would be intense. The slamming doors near drove me bonkers but I would adjust. I could not stand to hear other guards call the inmates by their last names or even call me Acoose; but I adjusted. It was just easier remembering last names now that I have it all figured out. It was lonely though. Those ghosts were knocking pretty hard on the old heart I tell you. I had feelings that I cannot even tell you about. Some things are just too hard to express. However, I would never tell anyone about all this because I was not sure how it would be perceived. They might think me a pussy or something. Little bit of the old stuff here. You know Sharon centered, but full of old fear.

I did not know who to trust so the ghosts had to be kept silent. As I said the training was weird and I almost did not make it. I passed by the skin of my teeth and I left the Masters program with a pretty fair GPA or grade point average. Very weird! I did have to write the exam over and at least I got that chance. You know what really got on my last nerve? Well our trainers kept telling us if we did not make it through the exam that we would not have a job. You know this shit wears on a body, but I never gave up. At least they were consistent. I made it. The uniforms were trippy. We dressed in gray and blue. Using the keys was another hurdle to cross because there were eighty-six of the motherfuckers on one chain. We had not really been trained to work these puppies but we would learn. It was nerve racking especially when you had a bunch of inmates waiting on you and you have your balls in your hand not knowing which one to use. It made you look dumb but it all worked out in the end. As a matter of a fact, I still have troubles today with my keys.

I heard so many horror stories about this joint. I thought to myself, "Okay what the fuck are ya doing now, trying to be a guard are we?" You know I never knew what I would do next and this was a good one. Wearing those cute little uniforms and hauling around those heavy keys, they were heavy enough to drop your draws, was honestly pretty cool. You know I have no idea why. I put all the bullshit behind me and ended up doing my own thing. I learned most of my shit by trial and error; mostly error I believe. Those who want change will change and those who do not will continue to be in jail. Simple.

I worked all three shifts; days, afternoons and nights. I hated those nights. My greatest fear was to find a man hanging. I thank my blessings it never happened. Shit like this happens all the time with inmates. The first few months were tough. I remember I use to walk out to the parking lot get in my vehicle and cry. I never let anyone see this. I refused to let anyone see that I had a weak side. You see I was letting people get to me, both inmates and staff. The negativity and bullshit almost played me. It was like putting a load right into your veins. I was letting words and actions of others rule my thoughts. I thought to myself, "Fuck it and everyone else. Don't let these motherfuckers win. Stand up and fight for yourself and be a good soldier. Hold your dignity." You know I did. I became a true and pure Warrior. I was rudely awakened and finally smelled the Java. Just like everything else in my life I never gave up. When I fell I'd just get up dust myself off and move on. I could not believe that I had let a select number of people get to me in this manner. Well I would not have it. I had not lived this long to let someone knock me down, not without a fight that is. It just was not me. I was again ready for battle as always. Come to think of it, I was born ready.

I then proceeded to take hold and I proved myself to be a worthy opponent. I did not take shit from that point on. I rubbed elbows with the right people and I made some friends. I mean really, I did not apply here to find anything but a career but having the odd bud is nice. It was great, weird but great. If people talked about me it was behind my back. NO one had the balls to say anything to me and God help them if I would have heard. I just happened to have bigger and heavier balls. Really I was quite proud of this. I mean I did not go around pushing my weight nor did I show off my balls but I did look after myself. I had to or the sharks would have devoured me. I did what I wanted without breaking any laws. I was worried that one of the guys might ask me to do something like bring in dope and then I would have to tell on him because I mean I am the guard and I cannot do anything illegal. Been there, done that. Know what I mean? It was cool though and I had nothing to fret. I mean, the thing is, I knew lots of those guys. Good lord I'd partied with them and would slept with a few of them, so it was natural for me to worry just a tad. However, to keep the story straight, this was all back in the day when I was wild and loose. I mean if you did all this and then turned your life around and then ended up working with these people, while they were locked up, would you not be worried? You know that you would be. Anyway it all turned out for the best.

I was never hassled. Once in a great while some guy would attempt to pull shit but I would just tell them to hit the fucking road or I would charge their ass. Didn't matter to me. I would do what I would have to do is all. I remember one day I was walking down the hall and I ran into my cousin, who is now deceased. He stopped dead in his tracks and eyeballed me for a while. He then said, "Holy fuck is that you Sharon? What the fuck do you have a guards uniform on for?" He just kept walking shaking his head in disbelief. He never even waited for my reply. But we would talk before he died. He actually asked me once how I managed to stay sober. He was wondering if I could help him and I said no problem. We never had the chance because he died of an overdose or something. The street would get to him before I could.

I was good to the guys; or I tried to be at least. While I did what was expected of me as a guard, I attempt to treat people how I wanted to be treated. The only people I cannot tolerate are the sex offenders. I had a big issue with this. Most likely from the sexual stuff I went through as a kid. The ghosts really tried coming to the surface but of course I won because I knew how to deal with it. My attitude really changed since working at the jail and it is not all good. However, the inmates will never con me because you cannot con a con; a few tired and they all failed. There are times I just hate them especially the men who abuse their women. Fuck I hate that. The thing is the women will do what they have to whether they are forced or not. It is a lifestyle that they have become accustomed to living. The women visit these buttheads week after and week and bring in drugs to satisfy their fuckhead old men. They take a risk of being jailed and they do not care. They only want to take care of their poor honey that is in jail. Why? This has always been my question. Must be love. Ha,ha,ha,ha,ha,ha.

I laugh heartily and out loud. Thing is once you been there it is hard to shut your eyes to what you see. I mean I was in love with the odd inmate and I would do stupid things like I have seen at the jail but dayum I still felt for those women who filtered in and out visiting. You just want to bitch slap these women and tell them to snap out of it; but it would likely be to no avail. You keep it buttoned and they do as they do. I did attempt to talk to some of the ladies who would visit, but I may as have been talking to the deaf. Not gonna happen when a broad is in love.

The guys would make me sick because I can see right through them. There are so many memories and so many ghosts. I didn't hate the inmates but I sure didn't like the way they were. They are always on the con, always. There was not a day that went by that a guy is not attempting to scam. I mean the day they step in the fucking door they are trying to get out. Fuck just stay out, duh! I mean there may be the odd guy who wants to change but not here not in this environment. It's that guard/inmate thing. We go through the motions and do the paperwork and that is it. If these guys were really serious about changing would they still be coming to jail? I think not. They have not yet surrendered to their evils, to their vices, and until they do they will be in jail. Regardless of all this I still attempted to be fair. I had to. I could not be an asshole because I have sat in jail. I know what it is like. I did all the same things as these men do and more. I am sure there was a guard somewhere that said the same things about me as I say about these noodle heads. I was no fucking choirgirl know what I mean?

Anyway, being a jail guard is a very interesting job. I have met a few good men and ladies in my co-workers. I did a story back in 1996 about my sorted past and my face was on the front page of the Leader Post. I had no idea that it was going to be like this. I thought I was going to be in the back section but no there I was front and center. It was quite the shock. I was a little worried at what the reaction would be at the jail I worked at but it turned out okay. I do not know if I was looked at different or what but no one treated me any different. Perhaps the respect was there that was not there before. I know I received many calls telling me that I did a good job. One guy at the Centre made a comment that had I been a white woman I would not have been on the front page or something. I have no idea at how he sees this as an Indian/White issue but he tried. It did not really matter. My buddy would not tell me who made the comment so I left it alone. Who gave a shit about what that asshole thought? Not me! It was only a story about a prostitute gone straight. I was the only one who cared and that is all that counted.

I did not do anything extraordinary, just my job. I raised a little hell every once in a while but it kept the place exciting. I was going to tell stories about certain situations but I think not. This book is not about looking at anyone's faults but my own. Most of the people I worked with were very cool. There are those who are not and I did my best not deal with them. I am an alcoholic so I stick with the winners because I choose to. I do not have time for bullshit. I have lived through a lot of shit why would I want to stay in it? I dealt with stuff as I am faced with it. I try not to throw any stones because I do not want them thrown back. Once in a while I get upset but I pray and let it go. I cannot control anything except my emotions and myself. If someone is a racist then so be it. I cannot change them nor can you so we move on and pray that one day they will see the light.

I was a guard for many years. I have had some bittersweet experiences but I have survived. After I made it through the bullshit I persevered. The experience has had its ups and downs. I mean where else can a woman have so many men and not have to put up with their bullshit. I can just lock the bastards up and walk away. What a relief, I love it. I loved my handcuffs even more. Okay, okay I'm just kidding. Gotta have some laughs. I have a few friends that I can say are my friends and that is all that matters. I mean in all my life being a guard was the last thing on my mind. I do not know if I made a difference for any of the inmates. Thing is I use to believe everyone can change, but you know I am not so sure anymore. I mean for sure I changed but I guess for those of us who don't change they just die or stay in prison. See I hated being in jail really but it was all I knew. Although on the occasion there have been one or two inmates who have asked me how I made it, and we talked. So maybe I did plant a seed and then maybe not?

For me this job is yet another hurdle that I have had to cross. The ghosts did surface. I have had to learn to look at the situation from a different perspective and so I have. For me it has been a success. I made my mark. I earned some respect. I found my dignity. I walked away from my pillars of salt. I made a new life for myself. There is no going back only moving forward. My job at the Correctional Centre (The Hill) was simply another stone I had to turn.

I am proud to be what I am because look at what I was. The ghosts have risen on many occasions but only to be crushed by the positivity of my wonderful life. The arrows in my heart would diminish one by one. My job as a guard was good. There are good times and sad times. As a matter of fact we just buried one of our brother's. I mean other guards have died but this young man was my friend. But he had to leave. I did not know how much he meant to me till I was at his funeral, and I have grieved. He was such a nerd but he was my friend. We argued a lot about really stupid things. I would call him a racist and the fight would be on. He worked nights because he could not do days. He hated them. Ah shit, he was a better night stalker anyway.

The Arrow In My Heart... Disappears

This one night I was standing out front, it was around 10:45 pm, waiting for my shift to start. I was pretty tired it being my fourth night and all I wanted to do was sit down. He came bouncing in with his cell phone in hand and a big ass smile.

I just looked at him, you know gave him that get the fuck out of my face kinda look, and I did look away. I actually walked away, but he bounced along behind me. He was very tall too. He was standing beside me looking down at me and I looked up and said, "What the fuck are you looking at?" He said, "Nothing" and laughed. I just stared at him. Then he said, "Look at my phone do you wanna see what it does?" I said, "No not fucking really." He said, "Ah come on look at this." He then called his cell phone from the phone in the hall and when it rang the thing lit-up all red or green or blue or some combination thereof and he was happier then a pig in shit. He was very mechanical that way with computers and shit like that. So anyway I just looked at him shook my head and walked into the Control Room and he followed me. He was bouncing along behind me saying, "Isn't that fucking great?" Really he was being all goofy and shit so I just said, "Please fuck off now." There were times we would do coffee runs and we would get into some pretty deep conversations. That it would take me off guard because I never suspected he felt anything. He just did not seem to have too many problems other than woman shit. Anyway he was one of the good ones and now he is gone.

Then there are some ladies. A nurse in particular that is not there anymore because she married some guy and moved on. I remember she had the damn cutest kids. As a matter of a fact she is the one I went to see Lou Diamond Phillips with and I paid $5.00 for a kiss. Hey by-the-by, I also seen Prince the sexy little mother. Then there was the lady I bought all the clothes from. She was like having a private vender all of my own. I use to buy furniture from her too. She was a pretty good chick to know. Actually at first I did not like her because I thought she was a fucking snob but I was very wrong. She was always teaching herself Spanish and she was pretty good at it I must say. She's cool. Then there was this little blonde who was an Acting Deputy Director (ADD). It took me a while to break her in but I finally did. I thought she was kind of snobby to but whence I started to talk with her I found out she was as fucking crazee as me. She was very supportive of me in certain situations and backed me 100%. We were friends and had a working relationship. I would tease her and call her my bitch. We sure did have fun. I mean really it is not that these people were snobby, it was just that the majority of them did not live like I did so of course they were straight johns; you know not street people. So I mean their perceptions would have been different than mine on a variety of things so you know, whatever.

An Arrow In My Heart

Then there is the parole officer chick and the one who lives in Moose Jaw, well she might not be there anymore, but I loved her too. Those broads were cool. Funny, all these people, once I got to know them, well, we just all had a good time. I mean yeah we worked in a jail but we weren't the ones locked up right? So we had a good time. These two ladies were very cool and I am pleased to know them. There are so many good people now that I think of it. What about that ADD with the salt/pepper hair and big tickler under his nose? This man has been instrumental in many things in my life. He always treated me with the utmost of respect. I remember one time he was so proud of me and really he was the only one who said anything about it. This one time at band camp – just kidding – really this one time at the hospital I tackled some big mooch who was attempting to steal the drug cart. I was watching one of the guys and we heard a ruckus in the hall so we went to investigate. I told my inmate not to move or I would kill him. So I open the door and I could see two or three people and one of them is yelling for security. I was always told never to leave your inmates alone so I turned around and cuffed mine to the bed I believe. Well I was under duress and did not know what to do. I stepped into the hall and looked at the situation and the orderly who was trying to put this guy down. He yelled at me to go get security. I was panicked but was thinking, and I thought okay so I'll go get someone. I'm dashing down the hall and I stopped dead in my tracks and said, "Hey wait a minute, I am fucking security." So I turned my tail around ran back down the hallway and jumped on the guy and helped the orderly to put him down. Then I pulled out my trusty cuffs and slapped them on this big critter. Done deal and wrapped like a pita. It was most exhilarating I must tell you. The hospital staff just thought I was great. I received letter of commendation from the hospital and even the police and of course my special ADD said great job Acoose. I love him. So that is my best experience ever as a guard.

I did make many good friends there and they are still my friends today. It was a crazy place to work though. You never knew what was going to happen one day to the next. I did lots of shifts in all the different areas and it was a great learning experience. I mean really a jail guard. And then there are the night stalkers and you know who you are. I loved those night guys well ok not all of them but some of them were ok in my books. Let me tell you about nights at the jail. You really gotta be a special kind of person to work nights as a regular shift. I could only handle them in small doses but I did them because really they were easy to do. There are only a select few night stalkers that I cared for and I really hope you know who you are because I cannot say your names. You are loved you silly bastards. Oh then there is the individual that assumed I was a Gang Member. ASSUME – means U make an Ass out of U and Me. But this individual made an ass out of themself. I really don't know where the fuck someone would pull out such a bizarre notion. I mean a fucking Gang Member of all things. It just took a long time to swallow and develop this one in my mind. It was hard to wrap my thoughts around it. I mean a Gang Member what the fuck? For that matter I have a lawyer friend and I could have gone after this individual for sparing with my good name, but I thought what the hell I'm still alive and that in itself will hinder this person. It is just one of those things that make you go hmmmmmmmm! A funny business. A fucking Gang Member – go figure? Let's just say it was an interesting job. I was a jail guard, yes I was.

The Cherry on Top of the Cake
The last thing I would do is a PhD. This was the bitch of all bitches. We talked about the undergrad and the master's degree now we have the PhD, the Cherry on top of the Cake. I started this venture back in 2003. I had been thinking of it for a long time and I was talking to a fellow faculty member and he gave me the name and number of my very first PhD Supervisor who was a very nice person. I went to see him and I had to write up a proposal of my reasoning as to why I wanted a PhD and at the College of Medicine – Department of Community Health & Epidemiology no less. I couldn't pick something more suiting oh no I had to go there but you know what I believe at the end of the day it picked me. I mean otherwise why would I be there?

I believe in destiny and I believe that all things happened for a reason for two. I mean we just don't survive, there are reasons why we live and why we die. I had to do this. I had to take on this PhD because there were non-believers outside my camp, and I had to prove to me, not them, that there was nothing that I could not do. I was like that little engine that could that never ever gave up the battle. I remember when I received the acceptance letter from the department I applied to and it said, "We are pleased to inform you that you have been accepted into the Department of Community Health & Epidemiology." I was so excited I showed my co-worker and close friend, I was insanely amazed. I stopped and looked at her and said, "What the fuck does Epidemiology mean?" And we had a damn good hardy laugh, you had to be there it was priceless. So, I started in August of 2003. My journey would be like a huge rollercoaster ride up and down up and down in and around. Man it was fierce and it nearly drove me to hiding the bodies really good. I never imagined I would actually do a PhD. I have always been a go getter even in my using days if there was money, drugs, alcohol and men to be got I got them all. I ventured into my PhD with an open heart and open mind. I knew what I was getting into but I had no idea how bloody intense it would be but then again I was in a pretty intense Department overall. It was like passing GO and not collecting my two hundred dollars. I just flew on by.

I would sit in my classes in awe and I would listen to the other students. There was I believe one other Indian woman who was in my classes and one other Indian woman was already done, gone and graduated. As I sat there I would look around the room and I would think dayum I'm there I have arrived and how the hell did I just get here well some things we will never know. Every once in a while I would feel my self-esteem take a nose dive and my self-worth would be lowered because for real I had no idea what the hell was going on, but I listened and I even participated as much as I could. I did try my absolute best but damn it was a bugger let me tell you. I knew at one point I had most assuredly bit off more than I could chew. But I was already three years in and my Band was shelling out the money for me to go and there was no way I could ever pay that back; so I kept on. I am not going to go into a big long story because lots happened during my PhD and maybe there can be another story for another time? Some of it was negative but this is not about bashing anyone, it's about how I was able to change my entire being and actually be successful in my life.

This PhD is about my survival, my will to live, my will to never give up even at the most difficult times. It's about getting and being right with myself. Looking in the mirror and feeling yeah you got this, you did it, you mastered a PhD. The years were tough. It took me eight and a half years, and the end was the worst. It was so close I could taste it and yet so far away from my reach. I would sit in office alone and I would cry. I would have a Smudge. I would pray and I would cry and I asked the Creator to either take me or help me to finish. I know my procedure was a bit unorthodox but I was stressed to the max. I was also helping my daughter look after her six kids and that was a trip. I could write a whole book about them and perhaps I will down the road. I also had to work fulltime. I did get some relief when I applied for a grant and was awarded a year off to finish up. I was given a year to finish and I only had to teach one class, and after that class man I went hard, like a dog in heat. I worked my tail feathers long and hard for hours. I could never do any work at home because of all the kids, so I just went in on weekends and I did my PhD in my office.

I would type into the night. I would be so tired I could have just screamed. I was like on fire. I had this burn, I had this intense feeling of just pushing myself to limits I didn't even know I was capable of. Sometimes I would just sit and stare at my computer for hours not knowing how to begin a sentence or how to end one. It was like I was standing on a glass floor looking through and I was trying not to have too much stress or I might break though that glass floor. It helped that I had "thee" best team of women you could have on your side. They were a combo of qualitative/quantitative researchers with so much knowledge about everything that it was not even funny. I mean I know they didn't know everything but what they had gave me the fire I needed to not give up. Dayum I get shivers just thinking about them and their intense support. It is a good world we just need to pick the winners and stick close. It's not easy in my world or the world I came from, but if I can do this let me be the first to tell you that there is nothing that you cannot do in this world. But you need to move your ass, ain't no one gonna move it for you. The team of women who were my PhD committee were my Angels. They gave me breadth. They never turned their backs on me ever but rather pulled me back from whatever stressor had me at the time. Most important is that they treated me as their equal. When you are an Indian in a White world it is not easy and especially being from the street well they didn't care. They treated me with respect and dignity.

As I said, my PhD took me eight and a half years from beginning to end. My defense was the best, well almost the best, part of this whole thing. The best part was the research I did with the Indian women I interviewed; that was the best. I was so afraid to go into my defense because I had heard horrible stories about students actually failing or having months of revisions to do, and well I didn't have months I had to get this thing done. I had invited my Elders, my daughter and niece came and even one of our MASW students came. It was awesome. We had a wee ceremony and Smudge before we proceeded with the defense. I believe in prayer. I believe that there is a power that is higher than me. I believe. These women, my co-workers, my family, my students all gave me the power I needed to get through. As I sat in my defense I was quite surprised really at how easy I was answering things. But then again, I did write the damn thing now didn't I? Of course I would be able to speak about it. It was so groovy. The defense took about an hour or so and I must say that External Reviewer was also another pretty damn awesome guy. He just made it so effortless for me to speak. I actually got mad a lil bit but it was all good no one got hurt. I will never forget how I felt that day, it was Sept 28th, 2012 and I passed my PhD defense with minor revisions. I had like five things to fix or something crazy but then again I had a kick ass editor too. That cost me over $1,600.00 but it was the best money I ever spent. I have already thanked all those involved in my PhD and I am forever in their debt.

Then the Convocation on June 6th, 2013 was the bomb. It was the absolute best thing ever. I had a very funny looking University of Saskatchewan (UofS) PhD gown, but you know what I rocked it nonetheless. My friend, her daughter and my granddaughter were with me.

Off we went to the Convocation. It was long and as I sat in that Auditorium I was so excited I could hardly contain myself. I was like a kid in a candy story. They finally called my name – Dr. Sharon Leslie Acoose – and as I crossed that stage it was like I was floating on top of the earth. It was surreal. Then to top it off they invited all PhD students to sit on stage with all the UofS big wigs and for me that was a Blessing, I was so bloody honored. I never felt so cool in all my life. I made it! I did the impossible for someone having lived on the street spending most of my life in and out of prison, prostituting, drugging, drinking and carrying on and on and on. I have me a PhD. The impossible. I have lived, I am free...

The Beginning...

So here we are at the end that is only the beginning. I do not want to say this is the end or the conclusion because it is not, it is just the beginning of my life and how much time I have left on this earth. The arrow that was in my heart is gone. I pulled it out and with that all the life behind me has been released into the wind. My spiritual, physical, mental and emotional being is intact. While not all my days are good, I make the best with what I have in the present. I live each day as if it were my last and I don't look back very much. But I do use my life experience as a tool to assist others in their recovery from whatever they are recovering from. I don't look at life through a glass anymore. Things are very clear. My path is set before me and my Creator has given me this chance in life to make others feel good about being alive.

I have an emotional tie to my world. I have done this and written this for my healing journey. I have shared my experience, strength and hope so that another addict can perhaps find solace in what I have written. We all have a story of some kind no matter how long we have suffered. And there is an end. For those who still suffer that simply means there is something in your life that you must dig deep to find and release. I can tell you this, once you have figured that out and totally surrendered the rest will follow. And you will be amazed at what you will be able to discover in your life. Yes, it will be difficult. You will need to pick the appropriate battle for you.

My recovery from alcohol, drugs, street life and incarceration has given me this outlook on life that is so amazing there are no words to express it except to just love it and I do. The arrow no longer pierces my heart. I have forgiven all those who have hurt me in my past and I hope that those I have hurt have also forgiven me; or at least try. I live each day as if it was my last day on earth and I honor the Creator of my understanding. So for those of you who are still out there, and still suffering, this is written for you. I pray that you find what I found... true surrender and love of yourself and your life. My last thought is that if I can clean up go back to school get three university degrees there is nothing that anyone cannot do, but you need to be spiritually, physically, emotionally and mentally balanced.

    I found my culture too and now I go to Sweats, talk and learn from Elders, I have one more Fasting Ceremony to finish off and I go to a variety of other ceremonies when I can. I had no idea at how rich my Saulteaux heritage really was and it is glorious. I Smudge and pray daily sometimes several times a day because of stress and what have you. I am so happy to have found my roots and happier to participate as part of my continued healing journey. I like to say that I have the best of both worlds. I come from the street and rose from the ashes to where I am today. The Arrow is no longer in my Heart because I have fought a long hard battle and won. I surrendered to my demons and the Arrow released itself from my soul. The Arrow in my Heart gave me life! *Hiy*! *Hiy*!

ABOUT THE AUTHOR

About The Author

Sharon Leslie Acoose, PhD (*Kiishiibii-biizuu-kinew-Ikew*, Circling Eagle Woman) is Associate Professor of Indigenous Social Work at First Nations University of Canada - Saskatoon Campus and Member, Sakimay First Nation. Dr. Acoose, a recovering addict with twenty-two years of sobriety, has extensive experience working with women and girls involved in prostitution and other violent issues that stem from living on the street. In addition to her academic career, Dr. Acoose currently runs a support group for formally incarcerated 'Indian' women.